Macmillan
English
Language Book

5

Mary Bowen

Louis Fidge

Liz Hocking

Wendy Wren

MACMILLAN

Scope and sequence: Units 1-9

	Theme	LANGUAGE BOOK 5		
		Reading and understanding	Vocabulary	Language building
Unit 1	**Water**	stimulus: *The Quest* text type: mystery story comprehension: multiple choice/extension	adjectives	abstract nouns
Unit 2	**Water**	stimulus: *The Water Cycle* text type: information/explanation comprehension: sequencing a process/extension	alphabetical order	phrases
Unit 3	**Adventures**	stimulus: *Cliffhanger* text type: adventure story comprehension: true or false/extension	root words	apostrophes – omission and possession
Unit 4	**Adventures**	stimulus: *Woodlands Adventure Park* text type: information/persuasive writing comprehension: cloze/inferential/personal response/extension	**or/er** words	adverbs from adjectives
		REVISION: UNITS 1-4		
Unit 5	**Mysteries**	stimulus: *The Mysterious Cupboard* text type: fantasy fiction story comprehension: narrative sequence/extension	homophones	adjectives with **y** and **ful**
Unit 6	**Mysteries**	stimulus: *The Mystery of the Mary Celeste* text type: interview comprehension: find the mistakes/inferential/extension	definitions	simple sentence; subject/verb/object
Unit 7	**Up in the sky**	stimulus: *Daedalus and Icarus* text type: play comprehension: multiple choice/extension	definitions	simple and compound sentences
Unit 8	**Up in the sky**	stimulus: *Man on the Moon* text type: newspaper report comprehension: true or false/extension	synonyms	phrasal verbs
Unit 9	**Up in the sky**	stimulus: *Soft landings/Moonlight/Spaceflight/Stars* text type: rhyming poetry/haikus comprehension: literal/inferential/extension	words with more than one meaning	**ing** adjectives
		REVISION: UNITS 5-9		

LANGUAGE BOOK 5	FLUENCY BOOK 5		LANGUAGE BOOK 5	
Grammar	**Fluency**	**Spelling**	**Writing**	**Reading for enrichment**
present simple and present continuous *The fisherman is mending his nets.* *He goes fishing every day.*	1 *Holidays*	suffix **ive**	continuing a story	*The Quest* (mystery story)
past simple and past continuous *While the plane was flying over the forest, John looked out of the window.*	2 *African explorers*	**tion** words	sequencing a process	*Water's for …* (poem)
present perfect and past simple *Have you ever seen a polar bear?* *Yes, I saw one yesterday.*	3 *Andes adventure*	**ent/ence** words	adventure story	*A Real-Life Adventure* (biography)
future **will**; first conditional *What will they do at the park?* *If the weather is fine, they will have a picnic.*	4 *Yellowstone National Park*	**ant/ance** words	letter writing	*What's an adventure race?* (personal recount)
REVISION: UNITS 1-4				
modal verbs – **should/ought to/must** *We should unpack the suitcases.* *We ought to empty the boxes.* *First we must have something to eat.*	5 *Going underground*	**ture** words	imaginative writing	*The caves at Wookey Hole* (information/ explanation)
present simple passive *The ship is sailed by the crew.* *Meals are cooked in the galley.*	6 *Mystery in Peru*	**gu** words	interview	*The Bermuda Triangle* (information)
conversational phrases – agreement *So do I. Me too.* *Neither do I. Me neither.*	7 *TV stars*	**ie** words	a play scene	*Wings* (information/ explanation)
present continuous with future meaning *Five astronauts are going to the moon tomorrow.* *Their rocket is taking off at 10am.*	8 *'KidzWorld' magazine*	**ei** words	newspaper report	*I want to be an astronaut* (poem)
exclamations and result clauses *It's so hot! It's such a hot day!* *They are such good players that they win every match.*	9 *The sky at night*	**tch** words	haikus	*Our Solar System* (information)
REVISION: UNITS 5-9				

Scope and sequence: Units 10-18

	Theme	LANGUAGE BOOK 5		
		Reading and understanding	Vocabulary	Language building
Unit 10	Exploration	stimulus: *The shipwreck* text type: narrative adventure story comprehension: multiple choice/extension	word definitions	direct speech (review)
Unit 11	Exploration	stimulus: *Exploring Greece* text type: summary notes/non-fiction report comprehension: correcting sentences/extension	definitions	forms of sentence
Unit 12	Environment	stimulus: *The Stream* text type: narrative adventure story comprehension: cloze exercise/extension	synonyms	future tense with **will**
Unit 13	Environment	stimulus: *Join World Watch* text type: persuasive writing in form of leaflet comprehension: true or false/extension	alphabetical order	active and passive verbs
		REVISION: UNITS 10-13		
Unit 14	Inventions	stimulus: *Kate is made smaller* text type: fantasy fiction story comprehension: multiple choice/extension	words and definitions/parts of speech	gender
Unit 15	Inventions	stimulus: *Television* text type: biography/expressing a point of view comprehension: literal comprehension questions/extension	homophones	more about compound sentences and clauses
Unit 16	The Senses	stimulus: *A night in the jungle* text type: narrative story comprehension: sequencing/extension	synonyms/antonyms	reported speech (review)
Unit 17	The Senses	stimulus: *How your ear works* text type: explanatory text and diagrams comprehension: matching sentence beginnings and endings/extension	root words	changing verbs to nouns by suffixing
Unit 18	The Senses	stimulus: *The Five Senses Shop* text type: list poems comprehension: literal comprehension questions/extension	onomatopoeia	separating sentence tags with commas
		REVISION: UNITS 14-18		

LANGUAGE BOOK 5	FLUENCY BOOK 5		LANGUAGE BOOK 5	
Grammar	**Fluency**	**Spelling**	**Writing**	**Reading for enrichment**
reported speech (time shift present to past) *'I'm tired.' Jim said that he was tired.* *'I can't swim.' The girl said that she couldn't swim.*	10 *Ocean explorers*	two-syllable words – first syllable a long vowel	continuing a story (in chapters)	*The Dolphin* (poem)
past simple passive *The stadium was rebuilt in 1869.* *The Olympic Games were held there in 1896.*	11 *Journey in Greece*	words in which **ci/ti** sound like **sh**	non-fiction report	*Marco Polo* (biography)
present perfect + **for/since** *He has lived there for years.* *They have been on their farm since 1999.*	12 *'The River'*	words with same letter sound but different letter pattern	story settings	*How to make a solar still* (instructional text)
present perfect continuous + **for/since** *She has been in Borneo since 1995.* *People have been cutting down trees for years.*	13 *Let's recycle!*	suffixes **ful/less**	persuasive writing – posters	*The litter song* (poem/song)
REVISION: UNITS 10-13				
reported commands *James told Kate to sit down.* *He told her not to touch the machine.*	14 *Interview with a star*	**wa** (sound of **a** is modified after **w**)	writing a story sequel	*Cat's eyes* (biography)
modal verbs **have to** (past, present, future) *They always have to work hard.* *Jenny had to give a talk last week.* *Suzy will have to give a talk tomorrow.*	15 *Children's TV*	words in which **i** sounds like **ee**	expressing a point of view	*Albert the TV addict* (story with a moral)
question tags *It's noisy, isn't it?* *They're not dangerous, are they?*	16 *Night animals*	prefixes **pre** and **mis**	characterisation	*Your five senses* (explanatory text)
used to to express the past *They used to live by the sea.* *He used to play on the beach.*	17 *Look here!*	**war/wor** words	explanatory texts and diagrams	*My Hands* (poem)
reflexive pronouns *I baked the cake myself.* *The boys are enjoying themselves.*	18 *The big quiz*	homophones	non-rhyming list poem	*The Old Man and the Strong Man* (trad story from Iran)
REVISION: UNITS 14-18				

Some characters you will meet in this book

This is **Wordsworth**. He knows a lot about words. He will help you with vocabulary activities.

Bernie the builder will help you with grammar. He will help you to build sentences correctly.

Captain Superspell is a great speller. She will be there to help you with spelling. She will teach you helpful spelling rules.

Penny Pen loves writing. She loves helping people, too. Penny is always around to help you with writing activities.

The Quest

This is the beginning of a mystery story. Daeng is a fisherman in Thailand. He goes fishing every day. At the moment he is in the harbour. He is getting ready to go out in his boat.

Daeng was worried. He looked up at the sky. It was clear and blue. He looked round him at the calm sea. There was no wind and the monsoon rains had not come yet. The monsoon would come soon. During the monsoon, there would be rain all day, every day, for weeks and weeks.

But today it was perfect weather for fishing. Daeng turned his eyes from the sky and looked at his boat. It was a good fishing boat. He listened to the noise of the engine. Everything was alright. Why was he worried?

Daeng looked at the boy who was sitting quietly in the bottom of the boat. The boy was mending some fishing nets. Lek was a good boy. He helped Daeng a lot. Lek was clever and he learnt fast.

'What is wrong?' Daeng said to himself. He looked at the sky again. 'I have been a fisherman here in Si Racha for many years. But I have never been frightened before. And I don't understand why I am frightened. There is no reason for my fear.'

When he had no money for food, Daeng often went fishing in bad weather. He sailed his boat when the waves in the rough sea were huge. And he had never been frightened. Today the sea was calm, but he was frightened.

'We'll look for fish close to Si Racha today,' Daeng said to the boy. Lek looked up. He was surprised.

'But the weather is good,' said Lek. 'There is no wind. Why don't you go further away from the beach? There are more fish away from land.'

'We'll stay here!' Daeng replied.

The boy said nothing. There was something wrong with Daeng today. Perhaps Daeng was worrying about his money problems. Daeng had bought the boat three months ago. It was very expensive.

Lek stood up and picked up the fishing net slowly.

* * * * *

Stimulus   mystery story

Daeng stopped the boat and looked at the water. There were no rocks here. There was no danger. But he could not forget the words of the fortune-teller yesterday.

'Be careful at sea,' the fortune-teller had told him. 'There is death in the sea.'

What did the fortune-teller mean? Who was going to die? How were they going to die? What was going to kill them? A storm? Was Daeng's boat going to sink?

* * * * *

'OK! The fishing net is in the water now!' Lek shouted to Daeng.

The boat moved slowly forward over the blue water.

Lek turned round and looked at Daeng. Daeng was worried.

'What is it?' asked Lek. 'Is everything OK?'

'I don't feel well,' Daeng said. 'We'll go back when we've pulled in the net. I'll be OK tomorrow.'

Suddenly the boat stopped moving.

Daeng leant over the side of the boat. He looked down into the water.

'The fishing net has caught on something!' he said.

Daeng went to the other side of the boat and looked into the water. 'I can't see anything,' he said.

'Are there any rocks here?' asked Lek.

Daeng shook his head. 'No, there aren't any rocks here.'

'What is it, then?' asked Lek.

'I don't know, but we've got to pull the net into the boat again!' Daeng was worried.

Lek looked at him. Something was wrong. Now Lek began to worry too. There were huge creatures in the sea. They could be dangerous. Was the fishing net caught on a sea creature? Lek put his hand in his pocket and touched his knife.

Comprehension

1 **Look back. Find the correct answers. Circle them.**

1 Daeng was   a a fisherman.   b a fortune-teller.
2 On that day the sea was   a rough.   b calm.
3 Daeng was   a worried.   b happy.
4 Daeng told Lek that   a he was worried.   b he didn't feel well.
5 When the fishing net got caught, Daeng said
     a 'It's caught on the rocks.'   b 'I can't see anything.'
6 Lek thought that the fishing net could be caught on
     a a creature.   b a knife.

2 **Discuss your answers to these questions.**

1 Why was Daeng worried?
2 Why did Lek think that Daeng was worried?
3 How do you know that Daeng was a brave fisherman?
4 Why do you think Daeng said, 'I don't feel very well.'?
5 What do you think the fishing net was caught on?

Vocabulary

1 **Find *adjectives* in the story which describe:**

1 the sky   c_____   b_____
2 the sea   c_____
3 the weather for fishing   p_____
4 the fishing boat   g_____   e_____
5 Lek   g_____   c_____

2 **Find *adjectives* which mean the opposite.**
Use the thesaurus on page 166.

1 calm   _____   2 perfect _____
3 good   _____   4 clever _____
5 expensive _____   6 well _____

Language building

Remember! A **noun** is a naming word.

a **boat**

the **boy**

Most **nouns** name things which you can touch, taste, hear, smell or see.

Some **nouns** name things you think or feel.

We call these **abstract nouns**.

Daeng is **frightened**. He feels **fear**.

There is no reason for my **fear**.

---

1 Tick ✔ the correct column.

	noun	abstract noun
1 sadness	_____	_____
2 engine	_____	_____
3 happiness	_____	_____
4 rocks	_____	_____
5 goodness	_____	_____

2 Match the *adjectives* and the *abstract nouns*.

adjective	abstract noun
1 frightened	a kindness
2 kind	b anger
3 angry	c darkness
4 dangerous	d fear
5 dark	e danger

1 _____ 2 _____ 3 _____ 4 _____ 5 _____

Grammar

Do you remember Daeng and Lek?

It is a beautiful day. The sun is shining and a warm breeze is blowing. Daeng, the fisherman, is sitting in his boat in the harbour. He is mending his nets. Lek is helping him. They are getting ready to go fishing.

Daeng goes fishing every day. Lek helps him. They go out in the boat early every morning and come back late in the afternoon. They work hard and always catch lots of fish.

1 Answer these questions.

1 What is Daeng doing this morning?
2 What is Lek doing?
3 What are Daeng and Lek doing?
4 What does Daeng do every day?
5 Do Daeng and Lek go fishing every morning or every evening?

2 Ask and answer about the text.

sun – shine — Is the sun shining? — Yes, it is.
birds – sing — Are the birds singing? — Yes, they are.

1 warm breeze – blow?
2 Daeng – sit – boat?
3 Daeng – mend – boat?
4 Daeng – help – Lek?
5 Daeng and Lek – fish?
6 they – get ready?

3 Ask and answer about the text.

Daeng – go fishing – every day? — Does Daeng go fishing every day? — Yes, he does.

Lek and Daeng – mend the nets? — Do Lek and Daeng mend the nets? — Yes, they do.

1 Lek – help Daeng – every day?
2 they – go out – every morning?
3 they – come back – in the afternoon?
4 they – go fishing – at night?
5 Daeng – work hard?
6 Daeng and Lek – catch – many fish?

Turn to Fluency Book 5 Programme 1.

Spelling

> The suffix **ive** can change a **noun** into an **adjective**.
>
> expense   Daeng's boat was very expens**ive**.
>
> noun = expense   adjective = **expensive**
>
>

1   **Do these word sums. Make the *adjectives*.**

1   expense   +   ive   =   <u>*expensive*</u>

2   mass   +   ive   =   _____

3   secret   +   ive   =   _____

4   act   +   ive   =   _____

2   **Read the words. Discuss what they mean. Use the dictionary pages.**

3   **Use the *adjectives* you have made to finish these sentences.**

1

The tree is _____.

2

This girl is _____.

3

The watch is _____.

4

This boy is lazy. He is not _____.

Class writing

Let's solve the mystery!

1
1 Daeng and Lek got the net free.
2 They pulled up the net.
3 In the net was something which was:
  • very heavy
  • very old
  • **not** valuable.

2
1 Discuss what you think was caught in the net.
2 Make a list on the board.
3 Choose the best idea.
4 Write it here.

3 **Write a paragraph together on the board.**

Think about and discuss:
1 How did Daeng and Lek manage to pull up the net?
   Was it difficult? Did they need help?

2 How did they feel as the net was coming up?
   Were they excited? Did they feel frightened?

3 What was in the net? What did it look like?

4 What did Daeng and Lek do? Were they pleased
   with what they caught? Were they disappointed?

5 What did they say to each other when:
  • they were pulling up the net?
  • they found what was inside?

Reading for enrichment

What did you think Daeng and Lek caught in the net? Read the next part of the story and find out.

1

'We must go backwards,' said Daeng. 'Then you can pull the net into the boat.'

Very slowly, Daeng reversed the boat.

'Can you pull the net in now?' he asked Lek.

Lek pulled the fishing net as hard as he could. But the fishing net still did not move. 'No!' Lek replied.

'Pull again!' Daeng told Lek.

Suddenly Lek shouted, 'Yes! It's coming!'

Daeng went quickly to the side of the boat and helped Lek. They started to pull the net into the boat.

'There are fish in the net!' Lek shouted. 'Look!'

Daeng looked into the net. He saw many silver fish there. But there was something else in the net. It was blue and white, and it was shining.

'What is that?' asked Daeng.

They pulled and pulled. At last, the fishing net lay in the bottom of the boat. Lek stepped forward and opened the net. He picked up the blue and white thing. It was a plate.

Lek started to laugh.

'We've caught a plate! An old plate. Shall I throw it back into the sea?' he asked Daeng.

'No, no, wait a minute!' said Daeng. 'Give it to me.'

Daeng looked at the plate carefully.

'I saw a picture of a plate like this in a newspaper,' he said. 'The plate was very old. It was worth a lot of money.'

'But how did it get into our net?' asked Lek.

Daeng put the plate down and began to put the fish into baskets. When he had finished, he spoke to Lek.

'Perhaps there is a wreck down there.'

'A what?' asked the boy.

'A wreck – you know, a ship which sank a long time ago,' explained Daeng. 'There are lots of wrecks of old ships in the Gulf of Thailand. Perhaps that is why the net got caught. It was caught on a ship at the bottom of the sea. And this plate came from the ship.'

The Water Cycle

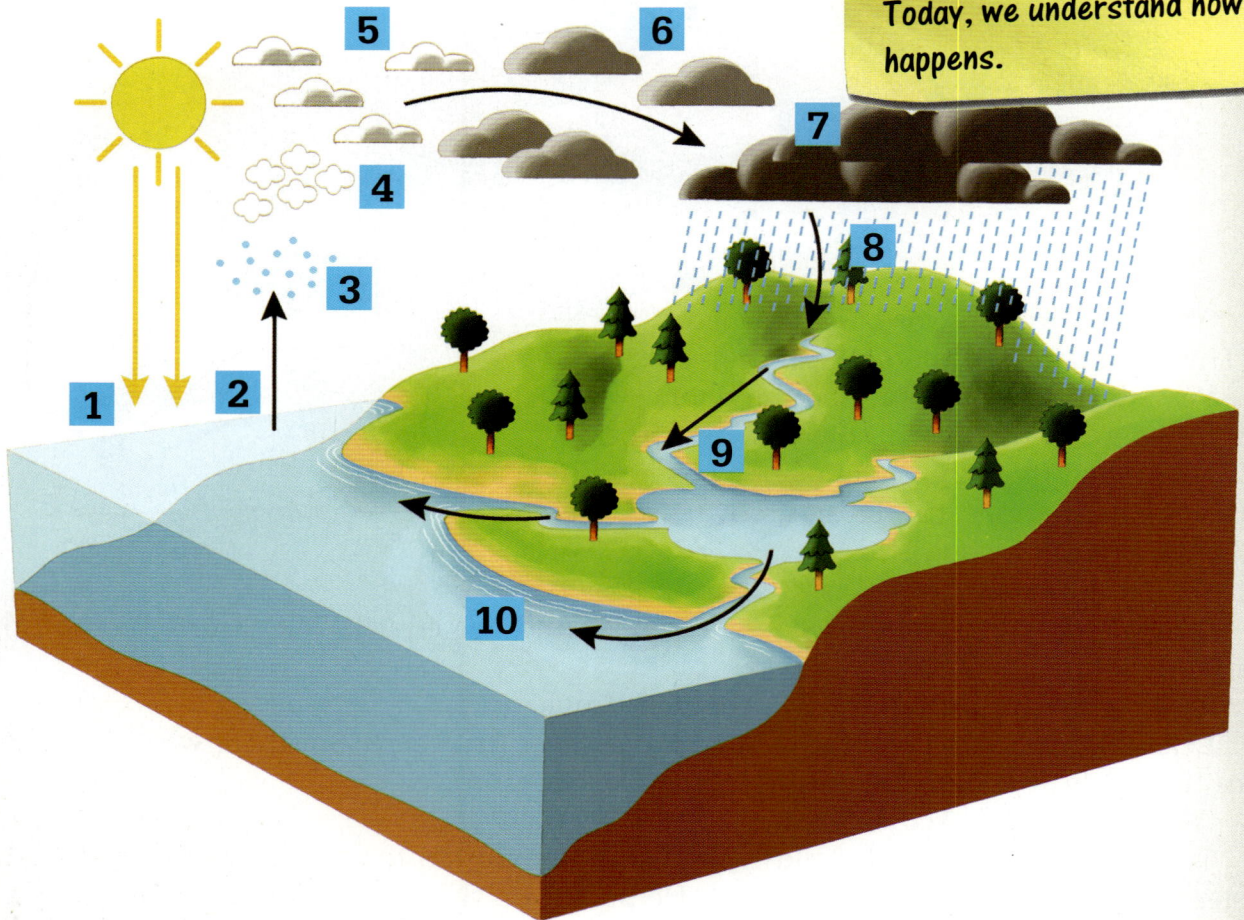

Step 1: The sun heats up the water in rivers, lakes and the sea.

Step 2: When the water gets warm enough, it becomes water vapour. This is called evaporation.

Step 3: The water vapour is very light and it rises into the sky.

Step 4: When it is high in the sky, the water vapour meets cooler air.

Step 5: As the water vapour cools, it condenses. It turns back into droplets of liquid which form clouds.

Step 6: The wind moves the clouds so some of them float above the land.

Step 7: When the droplets join together, they get big and heavy.

Step 8: They fall from the clouds as rain.

Step 9: The rain falls into rivers and lakes and flows back to the sea.

Step 10: While the water flows back to the sea, more clouds are forming in the sky.

Water vapour forms different types of clouds.

1

These clouds look like cotton wool. They are flat at the bottom. They usually mean that the weather will be fine.

2

These clouds are very tall. The top of this type of cloud spreads out. These are storm clouds.

3

These clouds are very wispy and form high up in the sky. They usually mean that the weather will be fine.

4

These clouds are flat and grey all over. They are very low in the sky and usually mean that it will rain.

5

A photographer was taking a picture of these storm clouds when lightning struck the tree.

Comprehension

1 **Number the sentences in the correct order.**

_____ When the water gets warm, it becomes water vapour.

__1__ The sun heats up water in rivers, lakes and seas.

_____ The wind moves the clouds. Some clouds float above the land.

_____ They fall as rain.

_____ The water vapour rises and meets cooler air.

_____ The water vapour forms clouds.

_____ The droplets join together and get big and heavy.

_____ The water vapour cools and turns back into droplets.

2 **Discuss the answers to these questions.**
Look at the pictures and information on page 17.

1 Which clouds
   a are wispy?   picture number _____
   b are flat at the bottom?   picture number _____
   c are very tall?   picture number _____
   d are flat and grey?   picture number _____

2 Which clouds
   a usually mean the weather will be fine?   picture number _____
   b are storm clouds?   picture number _____
   c usually mean that it will rain?   picture number _____

Vocabulary

1 **Write each set of words in _alphabetical order_.**

1 sun	sea	storm	sky
_____	_____	_____	_____
2 rain	rivers	rained	rises
_____	_____	_____	_____
3 cooler	cloud	coming	cools
_____	_____	_____	_____
4 top	this	tall	today
_____	_____	_____	_____
5 weather	water	wind	wispy
_____	_____	_____	_____

Language building

A **phrase** is a group of words which forms part of a sentence.

These clouds look **like cotton wool**.

'like cotton wool' is a **phrase**.

A **phrase** does not make sense on its own.

1 **Complete these sentences. Choose a phrase from the box.**

> back to the sea   water vapour   droplets of liquid
> big and heavy   cooler air   the clouds

1 When water heats up, it turns into _____.

2 As water vapour rises, it meets _____.

3 When water vapour cools, it turns back into _____.

4 The wind moves _____.

5 When the droplets join together, they get _____.

6 Rain falls into rivers and lakes, and flows _____.

2 **Make up sentences using the phrases below.**

1 like cotton wool   2 storm clouds   3 very wispy   4 flat and grey

Grammar

> Look! Rain clouds are forming over the mountains.

While the small plane was flying over the rainforest, John looked out of the window. Below him colourful parrots were flying above the trees. Monkeys were swinging in the branches. Steam was rising in the tropical heat. As they were crossing a wide river, the plane turned to the north and John saw the mountains. Grey clouds were forming around their high peaks. Soon the plane was flying through thick clouds. A flash of lightning lit up the sky. Heavy rain started to fall. They were flying through a tropical storm!

1 Correct these sentences.

1 While the plane was flying over the city, John looked out of the window.
2 Because it was so cold, steam was rising from the trees.
3 The plane turned to the south as they were crossing a lake.
4 Clouds were forming around the bottom of the mountains.
5 It started to snow as they were flying through the clouds.

2 Answer these questions.

1 While the plane was flying over the rainforest, what animals did John see?
2 Why was steam rising from the trees?
3 What were forming around the mountain peaks?
4 What did John see while he was flying through the clouds?
5 What was the plane flying through?

3 Finish these sentences.

1 While John was flying over the rainforest, he _____.
2 When John saw the parrots, they _____.
3 When John saw the monkeys, they _____.
4 The plane was crossing a wide river when it _____.
5 A flash of lightning lit up the sky as the plane _____.

Now write the sentences.

> Turn to Fluency Book 5 Programme 2.

Grammar *past simple and past continuous*

Spelling

The letters **tion** on the end of a word sound like **shun**.

When water changes into water vapour, it is called evapora**tion**.

1 Match the words and pictures. Write the words.

station   frac**tion**   direc**tion**   invita**tion**

1

_____

2

_____

3 ¼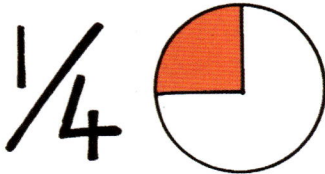

_____

4

_____

2 Add *tion* to these verbs to make nouns. Read the words.

Take off the **t** at the end of each word first!

1 collect   +   tion   =   _collection_____

2 protect   +   tion   =   _____

3 act   +   tion   =   _____

4 inspect   +   tion   =   _____

3 Read the words. Discuss what they mean. Use the dictionary pages.

Class writing

Look at the pictures.

1

2

3

4

5

6

1 Discuss what is happening in each picture.

2 Write about each picture together on the board.

Use the **present tense**.

evaporates	rises	condenses
cools	forms	flows

📘 Reading for enrichment

Water's for ...

Water's for ... washing, drinking
      making tea,
      cleaning the bath
      or scrubbing me;
      shining a car
      or rinsing a shirt,
      watering tomatoes,
      shifting the dirt
         ... my Mum says

But I say ...
      paddling in wellies
      or just in feet
      (puddles are good
      but the sea's a treat)
      squirting at brothers,
      splashing Dad,
      soaking my sister
      to make her mad!
      Mixing with mud
      to bake a pie,
      spraying the dog
      or catching a fly.
      Bath or puddle
      sleet or rain,
      let's play
      a WATER game!

Judith Nicholls

Words to help you

wellies	boots made of rubber which you wear in the rain
shifting	moving
a treat	something special
sleet	rain and snow falling together

Cliffhanger

Have you ever been on an adventure holiday? I went on an adventure holiday many years ago. This is where lots of children stay together in a camp and adults help them do lots of exciting things. In this story, Tim doesn't want to go on an adventure holiday but Tim's Dad has different ideas!

ADVENTURE HOLIDAY
FOR CHILDREN
lots of exciting activities....

NEWS TODAY

I knew I'd hate it. I kept telling and telling Dad but he wouldn't listen to me. He never does.

'I like the sound of this adventure holiday for children,' said Dad, pointing to the advert in the paper. 'Abseiling, canoeing, archery, mountain biking …'

'Sounds a bit dangerous to me,' said Mum.

I didn't say anything. I went on watching TV.

'How about it, Tim?' said Dad. 'What about an adventure holiday, eh?'

'You can't be serious! Tim's much too young,' said Mum.

I still didn't say anything. I went on watching TV. But my heart had started thumping under my T-shirt.

'He's nine, for goodness sake!' said Dad.

'But he's young for his age,' said Mum.

I still didn't say anything. I went on watching TV. I stared hard at the screen, wishing there was some way I could step inside.

'Tim?' said Dad.

I didn't look round quickly enough. Dad shouted. I jumped.

'Don't shout at him like that,' said Mum.

'I'm not shouting,' Dad shouted. He took a deep breath. He turned his lips up into a big smile. 'Now, Tim – you'd like to go on an adventure holiday, wouldn't you?'

Stimulus 🎧 *adventure story*

'He'd hate it,' said Mum.

'Let him answer for himself,' said Dad. He had hold of me by the shoulders.

'I – I don't really like adventures much, Dad,' I said.

Dad went on smiling but I think he wanted to give my shoulders a shake.

'Well, what do you like, Tim?' asked Dad.

'Watching TV,' I said.

Dad snorted.

'And drawing and reading and doing puzzles,' said Mum. 'And he comes top in all his lessons at school. Apart from games. You know he's hopeless at sport.'

'Only because he doesn't give it a try,' said Dad. 'I was Captain of football and cricket when I was a boy.'

Dad had tried to teach me football. Dad had tried to teach me cricket. He had tried and I had tried but it hadn't worked.

'Tim can't help being bad at games,' said Mum, pulling me away from Dad. She gave me a cuddle...

'I think an adventure holiday would do him the world of good,' said Dad.

He wouldn't listen to Mum. He wouldn't listen to me. He booked the adventure holiday.

'You'll love it when you get there,' said Dad over and over again.

He bought me new jeans and T-shirts and trainers and a stiff soldier's jacket to make me look tough. Mum bought me a special safety helmet to wear all the time to keep me safe. I didn't feel tough. I didn't feel safe.

I needed to hug Walter Bear very hard when Dad drove us to the Adventure Centre. Dad said I shouldn't take a teddy bear with me because the other kids might laugh at me.

Mum said I couldn't get to sleep without Walter Bear. I didn't say anything. I hugged Walter even harder, sniffing in his sweet, dusty smell.

'Look, Tim! I think that's it,' Dad said excitedly.

I didn't look. I shut my eyes tight. I hoped if I wished hard enough I'd somehow whizz through space and end up safe at home.

Comprehension

1 Circle true (T) or false (F).

1	Tim wanted to go on an adventure holiday.	T	F
2	Tim's Mum thought it was too dangerous.	T	F
3	Tim was good at cricket.	T	F
4	Tim came top in his lessons.	T	F
5	Mum bought Tim a safety helmet to make him feel tough.	T	F
6	Tim couldn't get to sleep without Walter Bear.	T	F

2 Discuss your answers to these questions.

1 Tim tells us, 'My heart had started thumping under my T-shirt.' How do you think he was feeling?

2 How do you know Tim and his Dad are very different?

3 Why do you think Tim's Dad wanted him to 'look tough'?

4 What sort of person do you think Tim's Mum is?

5 What sort of person do you think Tim's Dad is?

6 How do you think the story ends? Will Tim hate his adventure holiday? Will he enjoy himself?

Vocabulary

> We can add to the **beginning** or **end** of some words to make them **longer**. We call these words **root words**.
> root word = like   **dis**like   lik**ing**

1 Find *pairs of words* in the box that come from these root words.

hardest	unknown	smiling	hopeless	harder
safety	knowing	unsmiling	hoping	unsafe

1 hope _____ _____

2 safe _____ _____

3 hard _____ _____

4 smile _____ _____

5 know _____ _____

Language building

> **Remember!**
> We use an **apostrophe**:
>
> - when we miss out a letter or letters
>
>   'I **didn't** say anything.'
>
>   **didn't** = did not
>
> - for possessive nouns
>
> **Tim's** Dad booked the adventure holiday.
>
> **Tim's** Dad = the Dad belonging to Tim

1 **Write each of these as one word.**

I am	we are	I have	we have
he is	you are	he has	you have
she is	they are	she has	they have
it is		it has	

2 **Who is the *owner*? Write the answer.**

Remember the apostrophe!

1 Dad's newspaper   _Dad_   2 Tim's T-shirt   _____

3 the boy's shoulders   _____   4 the team's captain   _____

4 Tim's jeans   _____   5 the bear's dusty smell   _____

3 **Write each phrase with an *apostrophe*.**

1 the jacket belonging to the boy   _the boy's jacket_

2 the television belonging to the family   _____

3 the smile belonging to Dad   _____

4 the puzzle belonging to Tim   _____

5 the bear belonging to the boy   _____

Grammar

Uncle Bob has had lots of adventures.

Billy is talking to his Uncle Bob. Uncle Bob is a great traveller.

- Have you ever been to China, Uncle Bob?
  - Yes, I have. I went there last year.
- Have you ever climbed a mountain?
  - Yes, I have. I climbed Mount Everest two years ago.
- Have you ever seen a polar bear?
  - Yes. I saw one yesterday.
- Yesterday?
  - Yes, I was at the zoo!

1 **Ask and answer.**

… been abroad?   Have you ever been abroad?   Yes, I have.
OR   No, I haven't.

1 … flown in a plane?   2 … climbed a mountain?   3 … seen a dolphin?
4 … eaten Chinese food?   5 … ridden an elephant?   6 … heard a wolf?

2 **Look at this.**

 last summer   in 1998

two years ago   last winter

 two days ago   last month

Ask and answer about Uncle Bob.

Has he ever ridden an elephant?
Yes, he has. He rode an elephant in 1998.

1  2  3  4  5

3 **Answer these questions about Uncle Bob. Write in your copy books.**

1 Has he ever seen a dolphin? When did he see one?
2 Has he ever flown in a plane? When did he fly in one?
3 Has he ever heard a wolf? When did he hear one?

Turn to Fluency Book 5 Programme 3.

Spelling

Some **adjectives** end in **ent**. 🎧

Tim's Dad had differ**ent** ideas.

You can make these **adjectives** into **abstract nouns** by:
1 dropping the **ent**   =   differ ____
2 adding **ence**   =   differ**ence**

1 Complete each word. Write the words.

adjectives – add *ent*	abstract nouns – add *ence*
1 sil _ent_ _silent_	sil _ence_ _silence_
2 differ_____	differ_____
3 obedi _____	obedi _____
4 intellig_____	intellig _____
5 viol_____	viol _____

2 Read the words. Discuss what they mean. Use the dictionary pages.

3 Choose the correct word to complete each sentence. Write the word.

1 Tim was (silent/silence) when his Dad spoke to him._____
2 You cannot tell the (different/difference) between the two brothers. _____
3 An (obedient/obedience) child does as he is told._____
4 The children in the class were very (intelligent/intelligence). _____
5 The (violent/violence) of the storm was frightening. _____

Class writing

Every day Tim had an **adventure**. You are going to write about one adventure.

1 Discuss and choose one of these things to write about.

abseiling

canoeing

archery

mountain biking

Remember! The story is written in the **first person**. Imagine you are Tim.

Use **first person pronouns**   I   me   my

2 Begin the story on the board like this:

Today I did _____ . I didn't like it …

3 Finish the adventure. Discuss your ideas.

Your readers need to know:
- what you were doing. Describe the activity.
- why you didn't like it.
- how you felt before you started.
- how you felt when you finished.

4 Now write about the adventure on the board.

Reading for enrichment

A Real-Life Adventure

The highest mountain in the world is Mount Everest. It is 8,875 metres above the sea. The first two men to reach the top of Mount Everest were Edmund Hillary and Tensing Norgay. This is how they did it.

Mount Everest — South Summit 8748m

9. 8506m
8. 7866m
7. 7315m
6. 7010m
5. 6706m
4. Advance Base Camp 6462m
3. 6157m
2. 5913m
1. Base Camp 5455m

Steps in the attack on Mt. Everest

In 1953, a man called John Hunt took 200 men to the bottom of Mount Everest. He set up a base camp where some of the men stayed. The others climbed up the mountain for about 304.9 metres and set up another camp. Some men stayed behind and the others moved further up the mountain and set up a third camp. John Hunt did this until he had eight camps and he had reached 7,866.42 metres. Edmund Hillary, Tensing Norgay and a few other climbers went on to 8,506.71 metres. They set up camp nine. From here the two men started the last climb of 335.39 metres.

On May 29th, 1953, Edmund Hillary and Tensing Norgay had a breakfast of canned fish and lemon water. They left their tent at 6.30am to begin the climb. There was a strong wind and the weather was very cold. It was 80 degrees below freezing! At this height, there was not enough oxygen in the air to breathe easily so they had to take oxygen with them in heavy tanks.

They first had to cross a level area. They then reached a 152.45 metres snow slope. It took them until 9 o'clock to climb up the snow slope. After that, there was a sharp ridge of ice that seemed to go straight up into the sky. They used their axes and cut steps into the ice.

At the top of the ridge, they found a huge wall of rock. There seemed to be no way of climbing it but Hillary saw a crack in the rock. They got into the crack and pushed themselves up using their hands and feet.

After the wall, they came to what looked like lots of ice waves. They were very high and the two men had to cut steps in the ice to get over them. This took them two hours. When they climbed the last ridge, they were on a small, flat space. They looked around. There was nothing above them. This was the top of Mount Everest. They had made it! Hillary and Norgay were standing on the top of the world!

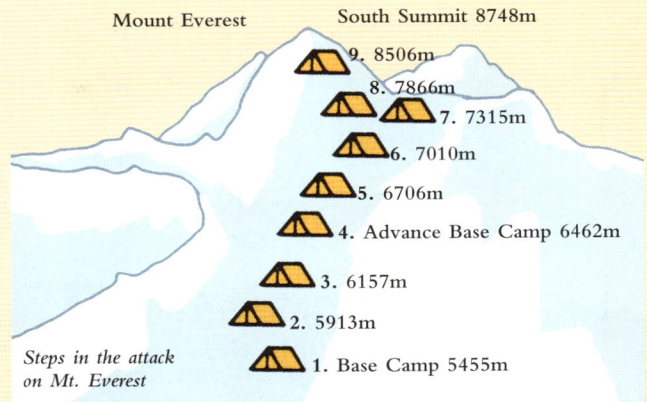

Woodlands Adventure Park

Fun for all the family at Woodlands Adventure Park!

Bring the family to Woodlands Adventure Park for an amazing day out! There is something for everyone to enjoy.

Choose from our many exciting activities!

- mountain biking
- canoeing
- sailing
- map reading
- driving a mini-tractor
- swimming
- water skiing

and many more!

Have a great day out! Remember – safety first!

- all activities suitable for beginners
- trained instructors
- friendly staff
- safety equipment provided

What our customers say about us.

Just a short note to say a big thank you for a wonderful day at Woodlands Adventure Park. I have never canoed before but it was great fun and the instructor made me feel very safe. If I have another few lessons, I will be very good at it!

Sally

What a brilliant day out! All the family enjoyed the mountain biking and the picnic in the woods. Our instructor knew all about the trees and flowers which we saw along the way. We certainly learnt a lot. If anyone asks us where to take the family for fun and adventure, we will say Woodlands Adventure Park!

The Green family

This was the best adventure day I have ever been on. I was a little worried as I am not a good swimmer but the instructor was marvellous. His kindness and patience made learning very easy.

Tom

New attraction!

This year we have a theatre under the trees. You can come to a magic show, a play, a puppet show – take your pick.

Get a leaflet from our information centre and see what's on.

Facilities at the Adventure Park
- free car parking
- information centre
- water-side cafe
- young children's supervised play area
- souvenir shop

Find us at Junction 22 on the M71
Contact us:
- by telephone on 0800 565565
- on the web at
  www.woodlandspark.org

Family tickets available.

Comprehension

1 **Complete these sentences with the correct word. Discuss your answers.**

1 There is something for everyone to enjoy at Woodlands _____ Park.
2 One of the things you can do is go _____ biking.
3 You can drive a mini- _____ .
4 All the activities are suitable for _____ .
5 Sally had not _____ before.
6 The Green family enjoyed a _____ in the woods.
7 The instructor knew all about the trees and _____ .
8 Tom is not a good _____ .

2 **Discuss your answers to these questions.**

1 Which activity would you choose? Why?
2 Why do you think 'safety equipment' is provided?
3 Why do you think the leaflet has letters from customers?
4 What does it mean when it says that the children's play area is 'supervised'?
5 What sort of things do you think you can buy in the souvenir shop?
6 Would you like to go to Woodlands Adventure Park? Why? Why not?

Vocabulary

An instructor instructs people.

1 **Write the word ending in *or* for a person who ...**

1 visits you   — — — — — — —
2 makes people better   — — — — — —
3 acts on the stage   — — — — —

2 **Write the word ending in *er* for a person who ...**

A swimmer swims.

1 runs   — — — — — —
2 bakes   — — — — —
3 farms   — — — — —
4 rides   — — — — —

Language building

Some **adverbs** are made by adding **ly** to an **adjective**.

We **certainly** learnt a lot.

adjective = certain   adverb = certain**ly**

1 Make these adjectives into *adverbs* by adding *ly*.
Discuss what each adverb means. Use each adverb in a sentence.

1 brave _____   2 wise _____
3 slow _____   4 correct _____
5 sad _____   6 safe _____

For some **adjectives** which end in **e**, drop the **e** before adding **ly**.

He was **simply** the best instructor I've ever had.

adjective = simpl**e**   adverb = simp**ly**

2 Make these adjectives into *adverbs* by adding *ly*.
Discuss what each adverb means. Use each adverb in a sentence.

1 sensible _____   2 gentle _____
3 horrible _____   4 feeble _____
5 true _____   6 terrible _____

If an **adjective** ends in **y**, change the **y** to **i** before adding **ly**.

It rained **heavily**.

adjective = hea**vy**   adverb = hea**vily**

3 Make these adjectives into adverbs by adding *ly*.
Discuss what each adverb means. Use each adverb in a sentence.

1 angry _____   2 happy _____
3 hungry _____   4 lazy _____
5 lucky _____   6 easy _____

Grammar

Do you remember Woodlands Adventure Park?

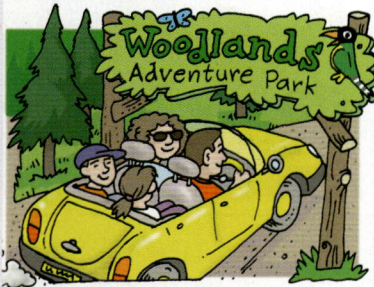

The Carter family are going to spend the day at Woodlands Adventure Park. What will they do there?

They will swim and sail. Molly will try water skiing and Tom will try canoeing. They will have a great time.

If the weather is fine, they will have a picnic in the woods. They will swim in the indoor pool if it rains.

1 **Name the sports at Woodlands Adventure Park.**

2 **Ask and answer.**

Will they do mountain biking?

Will they do archery?

Yes, they will.

No, they won't.

1 canoeing	2 water skiing	3 climbing
4 sailing	5 diving	6 swimming

3 **Read and make sentences.**

1 If an instructor helps her, …
2 Tom will be good at canoeing …
3 If it is a nice day, …
4 They will have lunch inside …
5 They will buy some souvenirs …

a if he has a few more lessons.
b if it is raining.
c if the shop is open.
d Molly will soon learn to water ski.
e they will have a picnic in the woods.

4 **Finish these sentences.**

1 The Carters will have a good time if _____ .
2 If Molly tries hard, _____ .
3 Tom won't do canoeing if _____ .

Turn to Fluency Book 5 Programme 4.

Spelling

Some **adjectives** end in **ant**. 🎧

What a brilli**ant** day out!

You can make these **adjectives** into **abstract nouns** by:

1 dropping the **ant**	=	brilli _____
2 adding **ance**	=	brilli**ance**

1 Complete each word. Write the words.

adjectives – add *ant*	**abstract nouns – add *ance***
1 brilli_____	brilli_____
2 import _____	import _____
3 assist _____	assist _____
4 dist _____	dist _____
5 eleg _____	eleg _____

2 Read the words. Discuss what they mean. Use the dictionary pages.

3 Choose the correct word to complete each sentence. Write the word.

1 We had to shade our eyes from the (brilliant/brilliance) of the sun. _____

2 An (important/importance) letter arrived this morning. _____

3 The shop (assistant/assistance) was very helpful. _____

4 We could see Woodlands Adventure Park in the (distant/distance). _____

5 Her dress was very (elegant/elegance). _____

Class writing

Imagine you have been to Woodlands Adventure Park.

Write a **letter** to the park saying:
- what you did
- what you thought about it
- what other facilities you used
- what you thought about them
- what else you would like to do at the park.

1 Look at the leaflet on page 32. There is a list of things you can do at the park. Take a class vote on which activity you are going to write about.

Write the activity on the board.

2 Discuss and make notes on the board.

- Have you done this activity before?
- How did you feel about it?
- What equipment did you need?
- What was your instructor like?
- What did you do?
- How did you feel when you finished?

3 Look at the leaflet on page 33. There is a list of other facilities. Take a class vote on the facilities you are going to write about. You can choose more than one.

Write it/them on the board.

4 Discuss and make notes on the board.

- Did the facilities help you?
- Were they good/clean/safe?

5 Discuss what else you would like to do at the park.

6 Now write your letter to let the people at Woodland Adventure Park know that you had a great day out!

Reading for enrichment

What's an adventure race?

An adventure race is when lots of different sports are combined into one long race. Each team has four members and all four must finish together. This amazing race in China lasted four days. Read what one woman competitor wrote at the end of each day of the race.

Day 1: 50 kilometres on bicycles, on foot, on skates and by canoe. Each team had only two bicycles. The fastest runners did most of the running. That was 30 kilometres. After this we skated for 10 kilometres on skates with wide wheels. Finally, we paddled a canoe across a lake (another 10 kilometres!).

Day 2: 60 kilometres by canoe and on foot. We ran up and down a mountain, through a beautiful forest and two villages (20 kms). Next we went down a river in a canoe for 25 kilometres. The water was rough and it was raining! Lastly we ran for 15 kilometres through some rice fields. My feet are hurting very badly.

Day 3: 50 kilometres on bicycles and on foot. We had to ride 30 kilometres up a mountain. The stronger riders pulled the weaker riders with ropes. We were given water and food at the top of the mountain – then we all ran 20 kilometres down the mountain! Tonight I am exhausted!

Day 4: 77 kilometres by bicycle, canoe and on foot. A 12 kilometre run up a mountain and into a dark cave. Through the cave and then down the mountain on a rope. We cycled 50 kilometres, then paddled 12 kilometres in a canoe and finally finished with a three kilometre run. 13 of the 17 teams finished the race. My team finished tenth. Our time was 26 hours, 27 minutes and 53 seconds.

Revision 1

1 **Look at the picture.**
Have you ever been to an adventure park or a play park?
What can you do there?
Do you like outdoor activities or indoor activities?
Do you like water activities?

2 **Listen and read.** 🎧

3 **Read and answer.**
1 How many water activities are there? What are they?
2 How many activities don't use water? What are they?
3 How many different kinds of boats does Woodlands have? What are they?
4 Does Woodlands open on Thursdays?
5 If you go to Woodlands on Sunday, can you go on the mini-tractor?
6 Can you follow the nature trail if you visit Woodlands in June?
7 What is the weather like today?
8 Which day of the week is it?

Where are we?

I'm trying to find out!

We have ten canoes here. Only five people are canoeing this morning.

Can I go in a canoe, please?

We'll go sailing tomorrow if it's windy.

Woodlands is closed on Mondays.
Nature trail open May–October
Mini-tractor Wed–Sat only
Open tomorrow!

What happened?

was riding down the hill, en suddenly ell off!

Have you been here before?

es. I came ere last year.

Lots of children are swimming today.

The water in the pool is usually very warm.

4 Listen and say where the people are.

1 _____
2 _____
3 _____
4 _____
5 _____
6 _____

5 Listen again. Write sentences. What will these people do?

If it's windy tomorrow, …

If he puts on a lifejacket, …

If they take the path on the left, …

If he goes to the first aid centre, …

6 Act out the scene.

The Mysterious Cupboard

Tina and her family moved into a house in the country. It was a large, old house. Tina's bedroom was in the roof. It had sloping ceilings and a large cupboard.

Tina looked around. The bedroom was a cheerful yellow colour. Some of her furniture was in the room. Her bed was under the window and her bookshelf was behind the door. In the middle of the floor there was a large pile of boxes. Each box had a big label on it: 'TINA'S THINGS'.

'OK, Tina,' said Mum. 'We ought to spend this afternoon sorting out your things. We must empty all these boxes.'

'I didn't realise I had so much stuff!' said Tina. 'It will take a long time!'

'Well, if we open one box at a time, we won't get into a muddle,' said Mum. 'There's a big cupboard and most of your toys and games will go in there.'

Tina knelt down and opened the first box. 'This is full of books,' she said.

'That's easy, then,' said Mum. 'They'll all go on the bookshelf and then we can put the box outside and make more room.'

Tina began to stack the books on the bookshelf while Mum opened another box. 'There are all sorts of things in here,' she said. 'I thought I told you to throw out most of this stuff?'

Tina finished stacking the books. She began to pull things out of the box her mother had opened. There were old, battered teddy bears, jigsaws, games and a bucket and spade. 'You don't need any of these things,' said Mum.

'I know,' said Tina, 'but I'd like to keep them. Can we just put the box at the back of the cupboard?'

'Yes,' said Mum. 'Good idea.'

Everything was soon back in the box and Mum opened the door of the large, fitted cupboard. She crawled in. It was very dark inside and a few cobwebs dangled in her face. The floor felt hard and cold.

Stimulus *fantasy fiction story*

'Tina, put a chair in front of the cupboard door so that it doesn't swing shut,' Mum called out from inside the cupboard. Tina propped open the door with a chair and then began to push the box through the cupboard door. Mum pulled the box from inside and soon they got it in. 'Right,' said Mum. 'Now I'll just push it to the back of the cupboard.'

Tina wanted to see what it was like in the cupboard. She crawled in as Mum was pushing the box. She pushed and pushed but it didn't reach the back of the cupboard. 'This cupboard must be enormous!' she said. Tina crawled further in. She helped her Mum push the box.

'Be careful!' Mum warned.

'Mum,' said Tina. 'The floor isn't hard and cold anymore.'

'I know,' replied Mum. 'It feels powdery like sand!'

Tina and her Mum crawled further and further into the cupboard. There was more and more sand beneath their hands and feet and it seemed to be getting lighter.

'Look!' said Tina. 'I can see sunlight!' Mum and Tina crawled towards the light.

'Where are we?' asked Tina.

'Well,' said Mum, 'I think we are in a cave.' They soon found that they could stand up and they began to walk towards the light. The sand was thick and soft under their feet. Tina suddenly ran forward into the sunlight.

'It's a beach!' she cried, 'and look! There's the sea. It's so blue.'

Mum followed Tina into the sunlight. They were standing on a beautiful beach with golden sand and palm trees swaying in the breeze. 'How did we get here?' asked Tina softly.

'A more important question is – can we get back again?'

Comprehension

1 Number the sentences in the correct order.

_____ Tina propped open the door with a chair.
___1__ Tina and her family moved to a house in the country.
_____ Tina unpacked a box of books.
_____ Tina crawled into the cupboard.
_____ They decided to put one box at the back of the cupboard.
_____ They were on a beach.
_____ They got the box into the cupboard.
_____ Mum helped Tina to unpack her boxes.
_____ They crawled towards the sunlight.
_____ Mum crawled into the cupboard.

2 Discuss your answers to these questions.

1 Why do you think the boxes were labelled?
2 Why do you think Tina wanted to keep the things her Mum had told her to throw out?
3 Why did Tina's Mum think that the cupboard 'must be enormous'?
4 What unusual things did Tina and her Mum notice as they crawled in the cupboard?
5 At the end of the story, what is Tina's Mum worried about?

Vocabulary

Words that sound the same but have different meanings are called **homophones**.

beach   beech

1 Write the correct word. Use the dictionary pages to help you.

1 Would you dig a **hole** or a **whole**? _____
2 Can you swim in the **see** or the **sea**? _____
3 Do you **meet** or **meat** your friends? _____
4 Do you **write** or **right** with a pencil? _____
5 Do you brush your **hare** or **hair**? _____
6 Can you eat a **pair** or a **pear**? _____

Comprehension; Vocabulary   *narrative sequence/extension; homophones*

Language building

We can make **adjectives** from some **nouns** by adding **y**.

'It feels **powdery** like sand.'

noun = powder   adjective = powder**y**

1 Make these *nouns* into *adjectives* by adding *y*.
Discuss what each adjective means. Make up some sentences and use the adjectives in them.

1 smell _____   2 silver _____

3 dirt _____   4 wealth _____

5 grass _____   6 sand _____

We can also make **adjectives** from some **nouns** by adding **ful**.

'Be **careful**!'

noun = care   adjective = care**ful**

2 Make these *nouns* into *adjectives* by adding *ful*.
Discuss what each adjective means. Make up some sentences and use the adjectives in them.

1 hope _____   2 fear _____

3 truth _____   4 wonder _____

5 colour _____   6 pain _____

Grammar

Do you remember Tina and her mum?

Tina and her mum looked at the suitcases and the pile of boxes.
'We ought to unpack the suitcases,' said Mum, 'but I'm so tired.'
'What about the boxes?' asked Tina.
'Well, we should empty them,' said Mum, 'but let's do it later.'
'OK,' said Tina.
'It's a lovely day,' said Mum. 'Why don't we explore the garden?'
'That's a good idea,' said Tina.
'But first,' said Mum, 'We really must have something to eat.
I don't know about you, but I'm starving!'

1 What should Tina do? Use the words in the box.

have a drink   tidy   brush   wash   clean   go to bed   have something to eat

Her shoes are dirty.   She should clean them.

1 Her hands are dirty.   2 Her hair is a mess.   3 Her room is untidy.
4 She is hungry.   5 She is thirsty.   6 She is tired.

2 What must you do? Circle the correct answer.

1 You must speak   a politely   b impolitely   to your teachers.
2 You must hand in your homework   a late.   b on time.
3 You must   a make a noise   b speak quietly   in the library.
4 You must always   a run   b walk   in the corridors.
5 When your teacher comes in, you must   a stand up.   b shout.

3 Choose *ought to* or *must*. Say then write.

1 They _____ unpack the suitcases but they will do it later.
2 Tina _____ tidy her room but she'll have lunch first.
3 I'm so thirsty. I _____ have a glass of water.
4 You can play in the garden but you _____ not climb the trees.
5 Do you think we _____ paint the house red or blue?

Turn to Fluency Book 5 Programme 5.

Grammar   *modal verbs – **should, ought to, must***

Spelling

In words ending in **ture**, the sound is **cher**.

Some of her furni**ture** was in the room.

1 **Discuss and write what each word means. Use the dictionary pages.**

1 adven**ture** _____

2 cap**ture** _____

3 litera**ture** _____

4 frac**ture** _____

5 mix**ture** _____

2 **Choose the correct word. Write the word.**

| punc**ture** | vul**ture** | furni**ture** | pic**ture** |

1

2

3

4

Class writing

Imagine that you and your teacher found a **mysterious** cupboard in your new classroom!

1 **Why did you and your teacher go into the cupboard?**
Think of some ideas.
Vote on the best idea.
Write it on the board.

2 **Suggest some interesting adjectives to describe the cupboard.**
Write them on the board.

At this point in your story you noticed the floor changed. You could feel snow under your feet.

3 **Discuss these questions.**
How did you feel when you noticed the snow?
What did you say?
What did you do?
Write the best ideas on the board.

4 **What happened next?**
Did it get colder?
Did it get lighter?
Write what happened on the board.

5 **What was it like when you walked through the cupboard to the other side?**
Discuss the nouns and adjectives you could use to describe what you saw.
Write them on the board.

6 **Now use the notes you have made on the board and write the story of your mysterious cupboard.**

Reading for enrichment

The caves at Wookey Hole

Wookey Hole is a place in the south of England where you can see amazing caves.

How the caves were formed

About 400 million years ago the ocean covered this part of England. When the tiny creatures which lived in the ocean died, they sank to the bottom. Their shells mixed with sand and became rock. This happened over millions of years so the rock pile grew and grew.

When it rained the water began to wear some of the rock away. It made rivers and streams underground. The rivers and streams cut away some of the rock. Huge caves were formed.

What the caves were used for

50,000 years ago, men lived in the caves in Wookey Hole. They hunted bears and rhinos with stone weapons. Much later on, some other people lived in the cave. We know this because people have found bones and broken pottery.

The caves today

The caves are very popular with tourists. They have electric lights so you can see the enormous roof and the lakes that are down there. Divers have reached 60.98 metres down into the underground lakes but they have not reached the bottom yet!

The Mystery of the Mary Celeste

John Brown has a programme on the radio. He interviews people who have interesting things to talk about. This is his interview with Professor Dent. Professor Dent studies mysteries. He talked to John Brown about the mystery of the Mary Celeste.

ON AIR

John: Welcome, Professor Dent. You are here today to talk about the mystery of the Mary Celeste.

Professor: Yes, John. People have tried to guess what happened but nobody has solved this mystery. It is very interesting.

John: Let's begin with what the Mary Celeste was.

Professor: The Mary Celeste was a ship. It had two masts and it sailed across the Atlantic Ocean in the 19th Century. On one voyage, something very strange happened.

John: When was this?

Professor: It was on the 5th of December, 1872. A ship called the Dei Gratia found the Mary Celeste in the middle of the ocean.

John: What was so strange about that?

Professor: Well, it was just floating there. The captain of the Dei Gratia signalled to the Mary Celeste but there was no reply.

John: What did the captain do then?

Professor: He rowed over to the Mary Celeste with three other sailors. They climbed aboard the ship and that is when they discovered the mystery.

John: What did they find?

Professor: It was very quiet. They searched the ship but there was nobody on board. The ship wasn't damaged and there was plenty of food and water.

John: What did they do next?

Professor: This is where it gets even more mysterious. They went to the captain's cabin and they found some breakfast on the table. The breakfast was half eaten.

John: No sign of the captain?

Professor: No, there was nobody on the ship. In the galley, that's where the meals are cooked, there were pots of half-cooked food hanging over a dead fire.

John: Do you know what happened?

Professor: No, nobody knows. The captain of the Dei Gratia thought that there had been a mutiny. That's when the sailors don't obey orders.

John: Did he think the crew left the ship?

Professor: Yes, but the lifeboat was still there so how did they get off the ship? Did they jump overboard? Did another ship take them?

John: If the crew did leave, what happened to the captain?

Professor: Well, they found a knife. It had some blood on it so some people think that someone murdered the captain.

John: What do you think?

Professor: I think we will never know. Some mysteries are never solved.

John: Thank you, Professor. I hope you will come on the programme again and tell us about another unsolved mystery.

Professor: Thank you, John. I'd like that.

Comprehension

1 **Read and correct each sentence.**

1 John Brown is a Professor.
2 The Mary Celeste sailed across the Atlantic Ocean in the 20th Century.
3 The captain of the Dei Gratia did not signal to the Mary Celeste.
4 The captain took six sailors over to the Mary Celeste.
5 It was very noisy on the Mary Celeste.
6 The ship was damaged.
7 There was no food or water on board.
8 The meals were cooked in the captain's cabin.
9 The mystery of the Mary Celeste was solved.

2 **Discuss your answers to these questions.**

1 John Brown interviews people. Does he ask questions or answer them?
2 Why do you think the captain took three sailors with him when he rowed over to the ship?
3 Find three things that were 'strange' about the Mary Celeste.
4 How does the layout of the interview help you to know who is speaking?
5 What do you think happened on the Mary Celeste?

Vocabulary

If you find a word you do not understand, use a **dictionary** to help you.

1 **Find these words in the interview.**

1 mystery	2 voyage	3 signalled
4 damaged	5 overboard	6 solved

2 **Match each word you have found with the correct meaning.**

1 voyage	a broken or harmed
2 signalled	b over the ship's side
3 damaged	c found the answer to
4 overboard	d long journey by water
5 solved	e sent a message to

1 _____   2 _____   3 _____

4 _____   5 _____

Comprehension; Vocabulary   *find the mistakes/inferential/extension; definitions*

Language building

A **simple sentence** has:
* a **subject**
* a **verb**

A **simple sentence** is also called a **main clause**.

The <u>Mary Celeste</u> <u>was floating</u>.

subject   verb

1 **Discuss which is the *subject* and which is the *verb* in each sentence.**

1 Professor Dent arrived.
2 John Brown smiled.
3 The interview began.
4 The two men talked.
5 Lots of people listened.

ON AIR

A **simple sentence** (main clause) can also have an **object**.

The <u>sailors</u> <u>climbed</u> aboard the <u>ship</u>.

subject   verb   object

2 **Discuss which is the *subject*, which is the *verb* and which is the *object* in each sentence.**

1 The captain signalled to the Mary Celeste.
2 The sailors searched the ship.
3 The crew left the ship.
4 The sailors found pots of food.
5 John Brown thanked the Professor.

Grammar

There's no mystery about this ship!

Have you ever been on a sailing ship? This beautiful ship is used by tourists. They can spend a week or two on board. They can sunbathe on the deck and swim in the sea.

The ship is sailed by the captain and his crew. There are two masts. The sails are pulled up and down the masts with ropes. Below the deck there are cabins. The passengers sleep in these. There is a galley, too. Meals are cooked here by the chef. The food is delicious!

1 **Read and make sentences.**

1 The ship is used …
2 The ship is sailed …
3 The sails are pulled up and down …
4 Meals are cooked …

a … in the galley.
b … with ropes.
c … by tourists.
d … by the captain and his crew.

2 **Complete these sentences. Use the words in the box.**

taken   used
found   made
caught

1 Sailing boats like these are _____ in the Mediterranean.
2 They are _____ of wood.
3 Smaller boats are _____ by fishermen.
4 Sometimes an octopus is _____ in their nets.
5 The fish are _____ back to the harbour.

3 **Ask and answer. Where are these creatures found?**

Where are eagles found?

They are found in the …

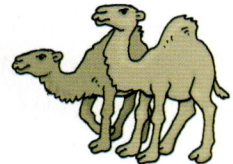

eagles   polar bears
parrots   camels

rainforest   mountains
desert   ice and snow

Turn to Fluency Book 5 Programme 6.

Grammar   *present simple passive*

Spelling

Some English words have the letters **gu** in them. The **u** is **silent**. You cannot hear it, but you have to remember that it is there.

People have tried to **guess** what happened.

1 Choose the word. Label the pictures.

| guess | guitar | guide dog | guide | guinea pig | guest |

1

_____

2

_____

3

_____

4

_____

5

_____

6

_____

2 Look up these words. Write their meanings. Use the dictionary pages.

1 catalo**gu**e _____

2 **gu**ilty _____

3 dis**gu**ise _____

4 va**gu**e _____

Class writing

John Brown is going to **interview** you!

1 The interviewer is John Brown. Choose one person from the class to be the interviewee.
Everyone can help with ideas.

2 Discuss these questions:
- What is John Brown interviewing you about?
Write your ideas on the board.
Choose the best one.

- What will he say to you at the beginning of the interview?

- What will you say to him at the beginning of the interview?

3 Think of questions he will ask you.
Write your ideas on the board.
Choose the best five questions.

4 Now discuss the answers.
Don't just say 'yes' or 'no'.
Make your answers interesting.
Write some interesting answers on the board.

5 What will John Brown say at the end of the interview?

6 What will you say at the end of the interview?

7 Now write your interview on the board.
Remember to set it out like a play.

Reading for enrichment

The Bermuda Triangle

The Bermuda Triangle is an area of sea in the Caribbean near America. You can see from the map that it is in the shape of a big triangle. Lots of ships and aeroplanes have mysteriously disappeared in this area. They have never been heard of or seen since.

For example, in December 1945 five aeroplanes flew over the Bermuda Triangle. None of them returned. They all disappeared! No-one knows where they went. There was no sign of wreckage and no SOS messages from any of the pilots. An SOS message is when a plane or a ship signals for help.

In 1976 a huge oil tanker was sailing through the Bermuda Triangle. It reported that the weather was very bad. Then the radio stopped and the ship disappeared without trace.

People have suggested different reasons for the disappearing ships and planes. Some people believe that there are magnetic rocks under the sea. The magnetism from the rocks makes the compasses in ships and planes go wrong.

Some other people believe that the seas are very dangerous in the area and that the weather is often very bad. Without a compass, planes and ships can get lost in bad weather.

Some people even believe that aliens from another planet come down and take the ships and planes back to their planet!

One thing is certain – the mystery is still unsolved.

Daedalus and Icarus

Characters

Narrator: the story teller
Daedalus: a famous builder
Icarus: his son

This is a very old story about a young boy who disobeyed his father and got into lots of trouble!

Scene 1

A room in the tower.
(The stage is dark. The curtains are closed. A spotlight lights up the centre of the stage. The narrator steps through the curtains.)

Narrator: Daedalus was a famous builder. The King of Crete had a problem he wanted Daedalus to solve. There was a monster in Crete and the King wanted Daedalus to build a maze. He wanted to put the monster in the middle of the maze so that it could not escape. Daedalus and his son Icarus went to Crete and built the maze. They then wanted to go home but the King wouldn't let them. They lived in a high tower and were watched whenever they went outside.

(Narrator goes back through the curtains. The curtains open. Daedalus and Icarus are in a room in the tower. There are tools and drawings all around, and a window in the back wall.)

Icarus: When can we go home, Father? I want to go home.

Daedalus: *(Putting his arm around the boy)* So do I, Son. So do I.

Icarus: *(Staring out of the window)* Look at the birds. They are free. They fly in the sky and come and go as they please. I don't want to stay here.

Daedalus: Neither do I, Son. Neither do I.

Icarus: *(Coming over to his father)* We have to do something but I don't know what.

Daedalus: *(Suddenly smiling)* You've given me an idea. I know what to do. Go outside and collect all the feathers you can find.

Icarus: What's the plan, Father? What are we going to do?

Daedalus: We are going to fly like the birds.

Icarus: Sounds a bit dangerous, Father. I hope it works.

Daedalus: Me too, Son. Me too!

Stimulus play

Scene 2
At the tower window and into the sky.

(The stage is dark. The curtains are closed. A spotlight lights up the centre of the stage. The narrator steps through the curtains.)

Narrator: Daedalus and Icarus made some wings out of the birds' feathers. They stuck the feathers together with wax.

(Narrator goes back through the curtains. The curtains open. Daedalus and Icarus are looking through the window at the audience. They are wearing huge wings.)

Daedalus: Remember what I told you. Don't fly too low. The spray from the sea will make your wings heavy. Don't fly too high. The sun will melt the wax.

Icarus: OK, Dad. I'll be fine. Let's go!

(They jump through the window onto the stage and 'fly' slowly across it. Icarus flies off the stage.)

Icarus: *(From off stage)* Look at me, Father. Look at me! I'm soaring!

Daedalus: That's too high, Icarus. Come down here with me! The sun will melt the wax and you will fall!

Icarus: *(From off stage)* What did you say, Father? I can't hear you!

Daedalus: *(shouting)* I said come down. You are flying much too near the sun!

Icarus: *(shouting)* Father! Father! My wings are melting! Pieces of my wings are falling off! I'm falling! Help! Help!

Daedalus: I'm coming, Icarus! I'll help you!

Comprehension

1 **Look back. Find the correct answers. Circle them.**

1 Daedalus was
   a King of Crete. b a builder. c a monster.
2 The King wanted Daedalus to build
   a a maze. b a tower. c wings.
3 Icarus wanted to
   a play in the maze. b go outside. c go home.
4 Icarus looked out of the window at
   a the maze. b the birds. c the King.
5 Daedalus's plan was to
   a climb down the tower. b speak to the King. c fly like the birds.
6 Icarus thought the plan was
   a silly. b dangerous. c fun.

2 **Discuss your answers to these questions.**

1 Why do you think the King would not let Daedalus and Icarus go home?
2 Why do you think the King wanted to put the monster in the maze?
3 Do you think Daedalus's plan was a good one? Why? Why not?
4 What advice did Daedalus give to his son?
5 Did Icarus obey his father?
6 Do you think Icarus was wise or foolish?

Vocabulary

The **dictionary** pages will help you with this.

1 **Find these words in the play. Write the words.**

1 This word begins with **p**. It is something which is difficult to solve.
   _____

2 This word begins with **e**. It means 'to get away from'. _____
3 This word begins with **o**. It is the opposite of 'inside'. _____
4 This word begins with **b**. They are creatures that can fly. _____
5 This word begins with **h**. It is the opposite of 'low'. _____
6 This word begins with **m**. It means to turn into liquid by heating. _____

| *Comprehension; Vocabulary* | *multiple choice/extension; definitions*

Language building

Remember!
A **simple sentence** is made up of **one main clause**.

A **compound sentence** is made up of **two or more simple sentences**. These simple sentences are joined by the **conjunctions**:

and   but   or

Simple sentence	=	Daedalus was a builder.
Simple sentence	=	Icarus was his son.
Compound sentence	=	Daedalus was a builder **and** Icarus was his son.

Simple sentence	=	They wanted to go home.
Simple sentence	=	The King kept them in the tower.
Compound sentence	=	They wanted to go home **but** the King kept them in the tower.

Simple sentence	=	They could try to escape.
Simple sentence	=	They could stay in the tower.
Compound sentence	=	They could try to escape **or** they could stay in the tower.

1   **Make some compound sentences. Discuss whether to use the conjunction _and_, _but_ or _or_.**

1 The king of Crete sent for Daedalus. Icarus came with him.
2 The birds were free. Daedalus and Icarus were prisoners in the tower.
3 They wanted to go home. They didn't know how to escape.
4 They could stay in the tower. They could think of a plan.
5 Icarus went outside. He collected feathers.
6 The plan was dangerous. It might work.
7 Icarus mustn't fly too high. He mustn't fly too low.
8 The sun melted the wax. Icarus fell.

Grammar

Do you remember Daedalus and Icarus?

Daedalus and Icarus are talking in their tower.

- I want to go home, Father.
    - So do I.
- I don't want to stay here.
    - Neither do I.
- I am so homesick.
    - Me too.
- I don't like this place.
    - Me neither.

1 **You are Daedalus. Agree with Icarus. Use *So do I* or *Neither do I*.**

1 I want to escape.
2 I don't like the king.
3 I don't want to see the monster.
4 I hate this tower.
5 I dream about our home.
6 I don't feel happy.

2 **You are Icarus. Agree with Daedalus. Use *Me too* or *Me neither*.**

1 I miss our family.
2 I'm not happy here.
3 I'm not sleeping well.
4 I have terrible dreams.
5 I can't eat.
6 I feel ill.

3 **Read and match.**

1 Icarus doesn't like Crete.   ____   a Neither can I.
2 He wants to go home.   ____   b So did Jenny.
3 I'm so happy today!   ____   c So does Daedalus.
4 I can't speak Chinese.   ____   d Neither does his father.
5 I went shopping yesterday.   ____   e Neither did Jenny.
6 I didn't buy anything.   ____   f So am I.

4 **Complete these sentences.**
Then read and respond with a friend.

1 I like _____.
2 I don't like _____.

Turn to
Fluency Book 5
Programme 7.

Spelling

The letters **ie** in some words sound like **ee**.

Pieces of my wings are falling off!

1 Say these words. Discuss what they mean.

1 p**ie**ce   2 sh**ie**ld   3 ch**ie**f   4 th**ie**f   5 f**ie**ld

2 Match each word to the correct picture. Write the word.

1 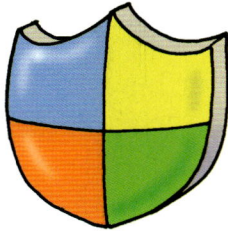   2    3

_____   _____   _____

4    5

_____   _____

3 Sort the letters. Write the words. Check the spelling with the words in Activity 1.

1 eldish _____   2 feiht _____   3 cfihe _____

4 ldife _____   5 iepce _____

4 The word *friend* has the letters *ie* but they make a *short e* sound. Write a sentence using the word *friend*.

_____

Class writing

We are going to write the **next scene** of the play.

Remember that:
- Daedalus and Icarus made wings.
- they escaped from the tower by flying.
- Icarus flew too near the sun.
- the wax melted.
- he fell out of the sky.

Narrator: Daedalus flies down from the sky to look for his son. He meets two people and asks them if they have seen Icarus.

1 Discuss and make notes on the board.

- Who is the first character Daedalus meets?
- What is he doing?
- What does Daedalus say to him?
- He has not seen Icarus. What does he say?
- What does Daedalus say?

Narrator: Daedalus walks on, looking for his son.

2 Discuss and make notes on the board.

- Who is the second character Daedalus meets?
- What is she doing?
- What does Daedalus say to her?
- She has seen Icarus. What does she say?
- What does Daedalus say?

Narrator: Daedalus hurries off to find his son.

Now write the scene.

Reading for enrichment

Wings

Birds' wings are many shapes and sizes. Their bones are different from other animals. They are not solid so that makes them light. They are also very strong.

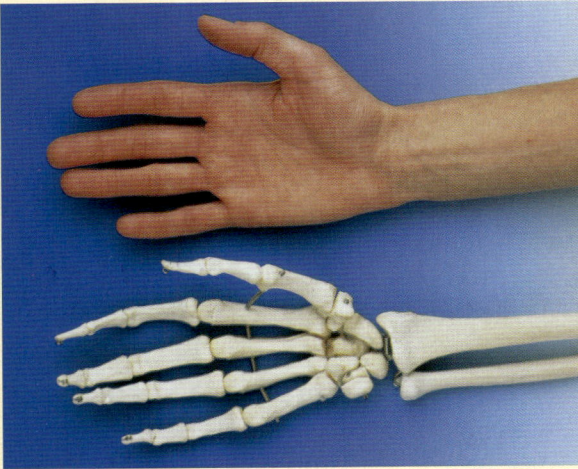

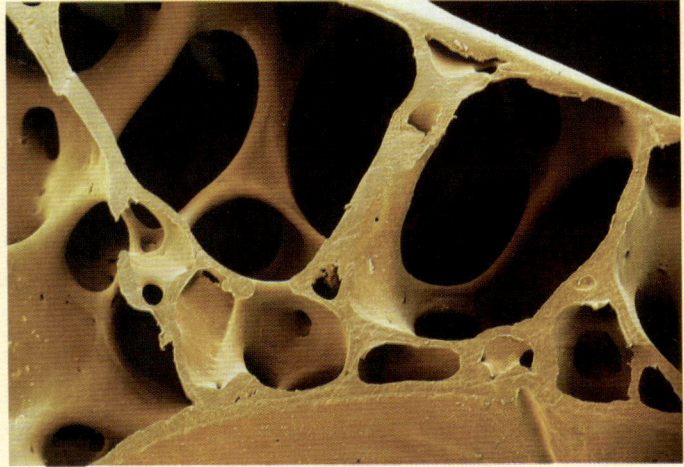

Long wings

Long wings help a bird to glide. The wandering albatross has very long, narrow wings. Its wingspan is 3.4 metres. It can glide over the sea for hours. It can even sleep while it is flying.

Short wings

Short wings are useful for changing direction quickly. The kingfisher lives near rivers and its short wings mean that it can twist and turn through branches of trees.

Wide wings

Wide wings are best for soaring. Birds of prey can soar high up into the sky and look down for food. The raptor can hover in one place for a long time until it spots its food.

The Daily RECORD

Man on the Moon

by John Barber

At 3.56 am today, July 21st, 1969, something that scientists once only dreamed about came true. Two American astronauts landed on the Moon in the spacecraft called the Eagle. They planted a flag and talked to the President by radio-telephone. Millions of people watched on television as the astronauts walked on the Moon's surface, 240,000 miles away.

This amazing journey to the Moon in Apollo 11, a space rocket, took three days and four hours. On board were three courageous astronauts: Michael Collins, Neil Armstrong and Buzz Aldrin. Michael Collins did not walk on the Moon but Neil Armstrong and Buzz Aldrin went into the tiny Eagle spacecraft and made the hazardous journey down to the Moon's surface.

The world watched and waited for six hours before the hatch opened and Neil Armstrong came out of the spacecraft. He was the first human being ever to step on the moon. He climbed down the ladder and jumped about three feet from the bottom step onto the surface of the Moon at 9.56 pm. His first words were: 'That's one small step for man, a giant leap for mankind.' It was almost incredible. A man was actually walking on the surface of the Moon! He went very carefully, almost shuffling.

The world heard him describe the Moon's surface: 'The surface is fine and powdered, like powdered charcoal to the soles of the feet. I can see the footprints of my boots in the fine sandy particles.' He then went to the side of the spacecraft and read the words written there. 'Here man first set foot on the Moon, July 1969. We came in peace for all mankind.'

Fifteen minutes later the second astronaut, Buzz Aldrin joined Armstrong on the Moon. His words were, 'Beautiful, beautiful, beautiful.' Aldrin began to move across the dusty surface of this strange, dead world. On Earth, both men weighed about 74 kilos but on the Moon they weighed a little over 11 kilos. Aldrin hopped like a kangaroo across the surface.

The astronauts then began their work. They had two hours in which to take photographs of each other, the Eagle and the landscape. They had buckets and spades with them to collect rocks and dust to bring back to Earth. Scientists could hardly wait to be the first to study rocks from another world.

After about two hours on the Moon's surface, the astronauts went back to the Eagle. A space scientist told us; 'They are resting now and are leaving the Moon in about five hours time.'

President Nixon spoke to the astronauts, saying 'All the people on earth are surely one in their pride of what you have done and one in their prayers that you will return safely.'

For the first time in mankind's history, men have left the Earth and walked on another world. They have looked at their own planet from a quarter of a million miles away. What was once a dream has actually happened.

Neil Armstrong on the Moon

Comprehension

1 **Circle true (T) or false (F).**

1	The astronauts landed on the moon in July.	T	F
2	Buzz Aldrin was the first man to walk on the moon.	T	F
3	The surface of the moon is like fine powder.	T	F
4	The astronauts weigh more on the moon than they do on Earth.	T	F
5	They had buckets and spades to make sand castles.	T	F
6	The astronauts walked on the moon for about two hours.	T	F

2 **Discuss your answers to these questions.**

1 Why do you think 'millions' of people watched the moon landing?
2 Michael Collins had to stay in Apollo 11. He did not walk on the moon. How do you think he felt?
3 How do you think Neil Armstrong felt when he first put his foot on the moon?
4 Would you like to travel in space? Why? Why not?

Vocabulary

Remember! A **synonym** is a word that means the same or nearly the same.

1 **Look back. Find these words in the newspaper report. Think of a *synonym* for each word. Use the thesaurus on page 166 to help you.**

1 amazing	_____	2 tiny	_____
3 hazardous	_____	4 giant	_____
5 carefully	_____	6 collect	_____

2 **Use each *synonym* in a sentence of your own.**

Now use the phrasal verbs in sentences of your own.

Language building

Remember!
A **verb** is a **doing** or **being** word.

Two American astronauts **landed** on the moon.
   landed = **doing verb**

They **were** on the moon for about two hours.
   were = **being verb**

We can add words like **of**, **up**, **down** and **of** after some verbs. This changes their meaning. These sorts of verbs are called **phrasal verbs**.

1 **Discuss the meaning of these** *phrasal verbs.*

1 When you **put off** doing something do you:
   a do it straight way?
   b do it later?

2 When you **speed up** do you:
   a go more quickly?
   b go more slowly?

3 When something **breaks down** does it:
   a go on working?
   b stop working?

4 When you **get rid of** something do you:
   a keep it?
   b throw it away?

5 When you **pull off** something do you:
   a succeed?
   b fail?

6 When you **come back** do you:
   a stay way?
   b return?

Grammar

Where do you think the rocket is going?

'Good morning, everyone, and welcome to CCB News, coming to you today from Space City.

As you can see, the rocket is ready for take-off but the astronauts are not here yet. They are arriving in two hours time. Five astronauts are making the journey to the moon, three men and two women. The experts tell us that the rocket is taking off at 10am. So be sure to join us later. You don't want to miss this!'

1 Answer these questions.

1 Is the rocket taking off now? _____
2 Will it take off later today? _____
3 Are the astronauts in the rocket? _____
4 When are they arriving? _____
5 How many astronauts are going to the moon? _____
6 When is the rocket taking off? _____

2 Look at the diary.
Discuss what the Watsons are doing on Friday and Saturday.

The Watson family

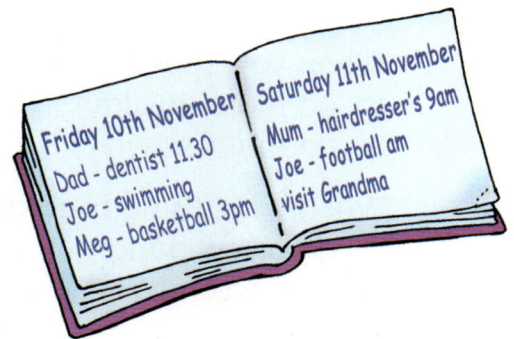

Friday 10th November
Dad - dentist 11.30
Joe - swimming
Meg - basketball 3pm

Saturday 11th November
Mum - hairdresser's 9am
Joe - football am
visit Grandma

3 Answer these questions.
Then ask and answer with a friend.

1 Where are you going after school? _____
2 What are you doing this evening? _____
3 What are you doing at the weekend? _____
4 Where are you going for your holidays? _____

Turn to
Fluency Book 5
Programme 8.

Grammar   *present continuous with future meaning*

Spelling

In some words **ei** sounds like **ay**.

On Earth, both men **weighed** about 74 kilos.

1 **Say these words. Discuss what they mean.**

1 **rei**ns	2 **ei**ght	3 **ei**ghteen
4 v**ei**n	5 **ei**ghty	6 w**ei**ght

2 **Match each word to the correct picture. Write the words.**

1

80

_____

2

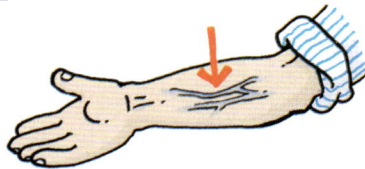

_____

3

8

_____

4

_____

5

_____

6

18

_____

3 **Use these words in sentences of your own.**

1 eight _____

2 weight _____

3 reins _____

4 eighty _____

Class writing

We read **newspapers** to find out what is happening in the world.
Here are some notes about the first man in space.

Name:	Yuri Gagarin
Age:	27 years old
Nationality:	Russian
Date of space flight:	April 12th, 1961
Launch site:	Baikonur, Russia
Name of spacecraft:	Vostock 1
What he did:	Orbited the Earth once
What he said:	'I see Earth. It's so beautiful.'
Speed in orbit:	27,400 kilometres per hour
Time in space:	1 hour 48 minutes
How he landed:	Ejected from spacecraft – used a parachute

Use the notes to write a **newspaper report** about the first man in space.

Look at the newspaper report on pages 66 and 67 again.

Discuss and write:

- the opening paragraph – what you will write to interest your readers.
- what you can tell your readers about Yuri Gagarin.
- what you can tell your readers about his space flight.
- how Yuri Gagarin came back to Earth and what happened to him.

Now think of:

| a good headline | a good illustration |

I want to be an astronaut

I want to be an astronaut
And shoot off into space;
I want to float like a silver bird
Above the human race.

I want to ride a rocket,
Computerised (with lights);
I want to go beyond the stars
I've seen on winter nights.

I want the Earth to watch me
On their TV screens;
I want them all to see me go
Amongst fantastic scenes.

I want to be an astronaut
And go to Saturn soon;
I want to step onto Mars
And the dark side of the Moon.

I want to spend my holidays
In a rocket that I'll fly;
I want to be an astronaut
Who waves our world goodbye.

I want to see the other worlds
And boys that aren't like me;
I want to see the strangest lands
And still be home for tea.

Peter Thabit Jones

Poetry

Soft landings

Space-man, space-man,
Blasting off the ground
With a wake of flame behind you
Swifter than passing sound.

Space-man, ace-man,
Shooting through the air
Twice round the moon and back
Simply because it's there.

Space-man, place-man,
Cruising through the skies
To plant your flags on landscapes
Unknown to human eyes.

Space-man, race-man,
Scorching back to earth –
To home and friends and everything
That gives your mission worth.

Howard Sergeant

Stimulus *rhyming poetry/haikus*

Haikus

Moonlight

Watch the shining moon
So bright in the midnight sky
A yellow round ball.

Spaceflight

Journey into space
Blasting off in a spaceship
Making such a noise.

Stars

Burning balls of fire
Dots of light in the dark sky
Fiery orange sun.

Comprehension

1 **Answer these questions about the 'Soft landings' poem.**

1 What is the space-man doing:
   a in the first verse? _____
   b in the second verse? _____
   c in the third verse? _____
   d in the fourth verse? _____

2 **Answer these questions about the haikus.**

1 How many lines are there in each haiku? _____
2 How many syllables are there in:
   a the first line? _____
   b the second line? _____
   c the third line? _____

3 **Discuss answers to these questions about the 'Soft landings' poem.**

1 In verse 1, how can you tell the space-man is travelling very fast?
2 In verse 2, what reason does the poem give for going to the moon?
3 In verse 3, what do you think 'unknown to human eyes' means?
4 Do you like or dislike the poem? Why?

Vocabulary

Some words have **more than one meaning**.
wake = **verb** meaning to stop sleeping:
         I **wake** at 7 o'clock.
wake = **noun** meaning a track moving
         behind something:
         I saw a **wake** of fire from the rocket.

1 **Find the *two meanings* of each of these words. Use the dictionary pages to help you.**

1 sound   a as an abstract noun   b as an adjective
2 plant   a as a noun   b as a verb
3 watch   a as a verb   b as a noun
4 orange   a as a noun   b as an adjective

Language building

> Remember!   **Adjectives** are describing words.
> **Verbs** are doing or being words.
>
> Verbs ending in **ing** can often be used as adjectives.
>
> The moon is **shining**. ←——— ing verb
>
> Watch the **shining** moon. ←—— ing adjective

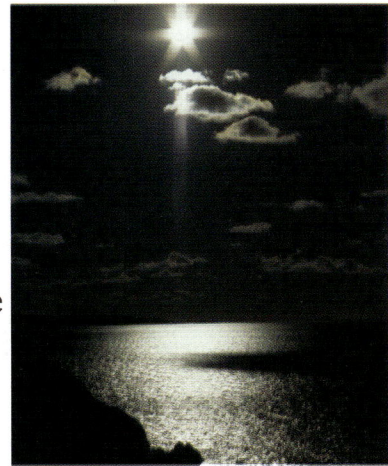

1 **Discuss whether the *ing* word in each sentence is a *verb* or an *adjective*.**

1. The space-man is **blasting** off the ground.
2. I saw a **shooting** star.
3. The sun is a **burning** ball of fire.
4. The spaceship was **making** such a noise.
5. The spaceship came down on the **landing** site.

2 **Make an *ing* adjective from each verb to complete each phrase.**
Make up some sentences and use the *phrases* in them. Write them in your copy books.

verb	*ing* adjective	phrase
1 to twinkle	_____	a _____ star
2 to roar	_____	a _____ spaceship
3 to set	_____	the _____ sun
4 to glow	_____	a _____ star
5 to return	_____	the _____ spaceship

Grammar

What can you see in the night sky?

Holly and her dad have come home late at night. Before they go inside, they look up at the sky.

- It's such a beautiful night!
    - Look at the stars! They're so pretty!
- They make such wonderful shapes in the sky!
    - There's a full moon.
- It's so bright that we can see everything in the garden.
    - But it's such a cold night that I'm shivering.
- Come on. Let's go inside.

1 **Make sentences with** *so*.

bright   *The moon is so bright!*

1
pretty

2
heavy

3
cold

4
old

2 **Make sentences with** *such a* **or** *such*.

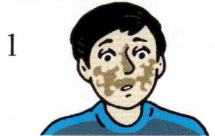
1   face! has a such He dirty got

_____

2   jewels are There the such crown! beautiful in

_____

3   good My is a cook! uncle such

_____

3 **Read and make sentences.**

1 The weather was so bad …
2 It was such an interesting film …
3 The boys were such good players …

a … that we watched it twice.
b … that they won the match.
c … that we had to go home.

Turn to Fluency Book 5 Programme 9.

Spelling

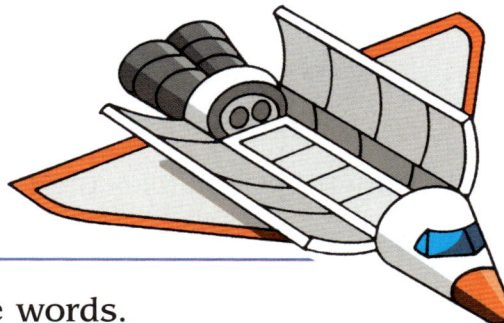

Some words have the letter pattern **tch**.

> The **hatch** opened.

1 Match the words and pictures. Write the words.

catch	match	patch
scratch	stretch	ditch

1

_____

2

_____

3

_____

4

_____

5

_____

6

_____

2 Make up some sentences using the *tch* words you have written.

3 Discuss the meaning of these *tch* words. Use the dictionary pages to help you.

snatch	sketch	fetch

4 Make up some sentences using these *tch* words.

Class writing

Read the **haikus** on page 75 again. We are going to write a class haiku about space.

1 Can you remember?

1 How many lines does a haiku have? _____

2 Does a haiku rhyme? _____

3 How many syllables are there in the first line? _____

4 How many syllables are there in the second line? _____

5 How many syllables are there in the third line? _____

2 Now think about your haiku.

1 Brainstorm and write nouns to do with space on the board.
   For example, rocket, stars, moon, emptiness, astronaut and sun.

2 Choose the idea you like the best.

3 Make a list of **adjectives** you can use to describe what you have
   chosen to write about.

4 **The first line:**

   Write your idea for the first line on the board.

   Count the syllables.

   Does it have five syllables?

   You may have to rewrite the line so you have **five syllables**.

5 **The second line:**

   Write your idea for the second line on the board.

   Count the syllables.

   Does it have seven syllables?

   You may have to rewrite the line so you have **seven syllables**.

6 **The third line:**

   Write your idea for the third line on the board.

   Count the syllables.

   Does it have five syllables?

   You may have to rewrite the line so you have **five syllables**.

7 Look at the **adjectives** you have used. Can you think of better ones?

8 Think of a **title** for your haiku.

Reading for enrichment

Our Solar System

Mercury
This planet is 60 million kilometres from the Sun. It takes 0.2 of a year to orbit the Sun. It is about the size of our Moon. It has a rocky surface covered in craters.

Venus
Venus is 110 million kilometres from the Sun. It takes 0.6 of a year to orbit the Sun. It is almost as big as the Earth. It is covered by thick black clouds of acid. The clouds trap the Sun's heat so it is very hot.

Earth
Earth is 150 million kilometres from the Sun. It takes 1 year to orbit the Sun. It is different to the other planets because it has water, oxygen and living things.

Mars
Mars is 230 million kilometres from the Sun. It takes 2 years to orbit the Sun. The surface of Mars is a cold, dry desert of red rocks. It has two small moons.

Jupiter
Jupiter is 780 million kilometres from the Sun. It takes 12 years to orbit the Sun. It is the largest planet and it is very cold. It is a huge ball of gas and it has 16 moons.

Saturn
Saturn is 1400 million kilometres from the Sun. It takes 30 years to orbit the Sun. It is made up of gases. The rings around it are rocks and ice.

Uranus
Uranus is 2900 million kilometres from the Sun. It takes 84 years to orbit the Sun. It is made up of gases. It is different from the other planets because it is lying on its side.

Neptune
Neptune is 4500 million kilometres from the Sun. It takes 160 years to orbit the Sun. Neptune is very like Uranus. There is a dark spot on the surface which is a storm about the size of earth.

Pluto
Pluto is 6000 million kilometres from the Sun. It takes 250 years to orbit the Sun. It is the smallest planet in our solar system. It is rocky and covered in ice.

Revision 2

1 **Look at the pictures.**
Does the planet look interesting or scary? Would you like to travel to a place like this? Why or why not?

2 **Listen and read.** 🎧

3 **Read and say.**
Picture a
1 What was in the space ship?
2 Which people work on Katz 2B?

Picture b
1 What is strange about Planet Katz?
2 What are the rings made of?

Picture c
Why do you think the space station is never left unguarded?

Picture d
How did Zak and Tom feel when they looked around? Why?

Picture e
1 What do you think *tremendous* means?
2 What things can you think of that roar?

Zak and Tom were on their way to Planet Katz. They were carrying supplies for the scientists at space station Katz 2B.

a **Hello, Katz 2B. We're arriving in twenty minutes.**

When Zak and Tom went outside, they had a surprise.

There's no one here!

c **Somebody ought to be here … Katz 2B is never left unguarded.**

Suddenly, a **tremendous** roar broke the silence.

Look over there, Zak!

e **What amazing colours!**

There was no reply from Katz 2B, but Zak had no time to worry about it.

It's such a strange planet. What are the rings made of?

A gas called Katzon. We're landing in one minute!

b

Zak and Tom looked around nervously, but they heard and saw nobody.

I don't like this!

Neither do I ... It's so quiet!

d

A strange rumbling sound began. The strange glow got brighter. Under their feet the ground began to shake.

Something's coming! What is it?

I don't know, but I think we're going to find out!

f

Picture f
1 Is a rumbling sound scary? Why or why not?
2 How does Tom know that something is coming?

4 **Listen and say which picture.**

1 _____
2 _____
3 _____
4 _____
5 _____
6 _____

5 **Act out the story.**

6 **Write what happens next.**

The shipwreck

Chapter 1 The storm

Thunder roared. Lightning lit up the sky. The wind howled. Enormous waves lifted the ship and threw it down onto the rocks near the mysterious island. There was an awful crashing, scraping noise. The rocks tore a huge hole in the side of the ship. Water poured into the hole. The ship slowly began to sink.

On board there was panic. 'Water is coming in!' yelled the cook. The news soon reached the captain. The captain shouted 'Abandon ship!' He said that the ship was sinking. People shouted and screamed. They rushed here and there. 'Get out of my way,' a sailor screamed. 'I want to get off this ship!' He pushed Jim in the back and knocked him over. He tried to lower a rowing boat into the sea to escape but there was no time. A huge wave washed him into the water. 'Help!' he cried as he disappeared over the side of the ship.

Jim stood up and held on tightly to the side of the ship. People were jumping into the sea to escape. 'Jump! Swim for your life!' shouted the captain. Jim took a deep breath and dived into the angry sea. Jim was an explorer. He left home to look for adventure – but this was more adventure than he wanted!

Jim saw the island in the distance. The waves splashed over him and dragged him down. He went under the water. He coughed and spluttered and gasped for breath but he kept swimming. Every minute he got more cold and more tired. He was terrified. 'I can't do it! I'm too cold! I'm too tired!' he thought. Just when he thought he could swim no further, he reached the beach.

Jim stood up and staggered up the beach away from the sea. He dropped onto the sand. The wind howled all round him – but he did not hear it. He was shivering with cold but he was so exhausted he went straight to sleep!

Chapter 2   The only survivor!

When he woke, the wind was quiet and the sea was calm again. The sun was shining in a clear blue sky. Jim looked around. All along the beach he could see broken wood from the ship. A few metres away he saw a wooden chest floating on the water. Jim grabbed it and pulled it onto the beach. When he opened it he found that it contained a hammer, an axe, some nails, a saw and some rope. Jim looked out to sea. There was no sign of the ship and no sign of any other survivors. Jim was all alone on an unknown island!

Luckily Jim found a stream where he could get fresh water. He bent down and drank thirstily. Nearby there were plenty of coconut and banana trees. He ate some bananas and broke open a hairy coconut with the hammer. He drank the sweet juice and ate the fresh white coconut. Then Jim sat down on a rock to think. He did not know if another ship would come past and rescue him. He did not know how long he would be on the island.

Chapter 3   Jim builds a shelter

The first thing Jim decided to do was to build a shelter. He needed to shelter from the sun and the rain. He didn't know if there were any wild animals on the island so he needed somewhere safe to sleep at night.

Jim gathered wood from the beach. He tied the wood together with rope and made the walls of a simple hut. He made the roof with tree branches and banana leaves. Jim gathered little branches and more banana leaves for a bed. He built a fence around the outside of his hut to keep out any wild animals. Now he had a shelter and somewhere safe to sleep!

Jim walked along the beach to look for other useful things. He found some of the ship's sail, a telescope, a knife and a leather map case. When he opened the case he looked in amazement. Inside was a map of the island! 'Now I can explore the island!' Jim thought.

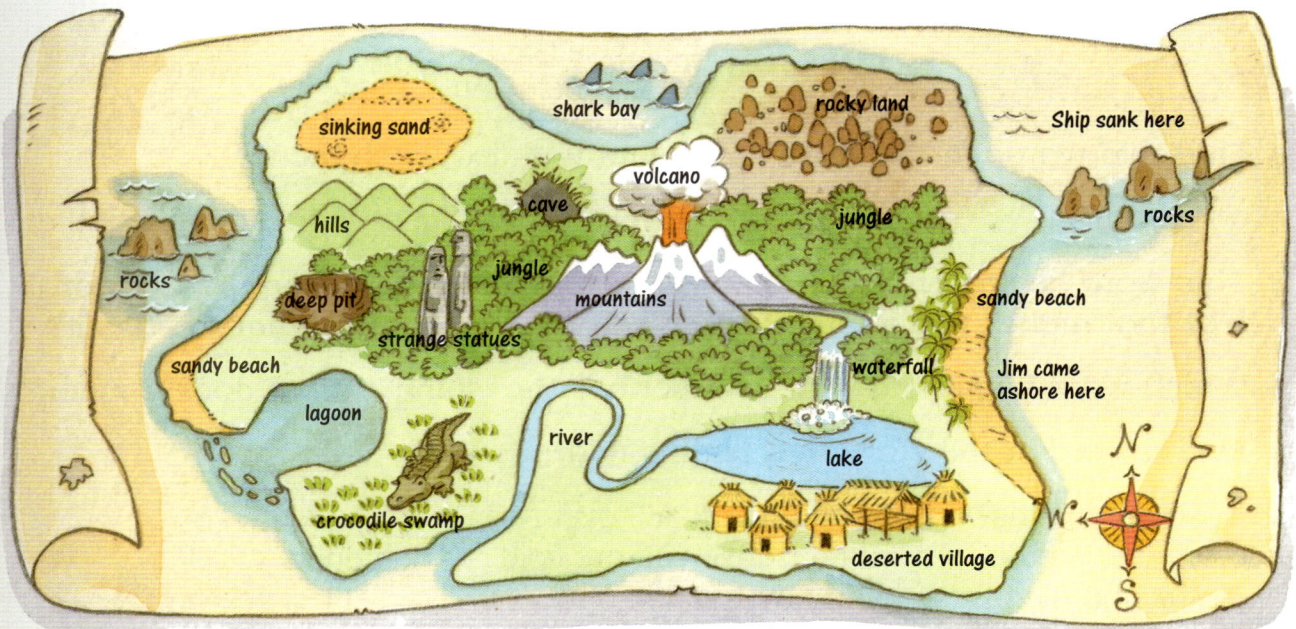

Comprehension

1 **Look back. Find the correct answers. Circle them.**

1 What was Jim?
   a a sailor   b a fisherman   c an explorer
2 What tore a hole in the side of the ship?
   a the captain   b some rocks   c the wind
3 How did Jim reach the island?
   a he went in a boat   b he swam   c he walked
4 What was the first thing Jim decided to do?
   a go home   b look for gold   c build a shelter
5 What was in the leather case?
   a a hammer   b a telescope   c a map of the island

2 **Discuss your answers to these questions.**

1 Why does it say the island was 'mysterious'?
2 How do you know that Jim was a good swimmer?
3 What do you think Jim thought when a he woke up?
                                       b he saw broken wood from the ship?
                                       c he discovered he was the only survivor?
4 What did Jim find in the wooden chest? How did these things help him?
5 Was it a good idea to build a shelter first?
6 What do you think Jim will find on the island?

Use the **dictionary** to help you.

Vocabulary

1 **Find two words in the story that begin with *ex* which mean:**

   a very tired   b someone who travels to new places to find out about them

2 **This word begins with *p*. It means 'a sudden strong feeling of worry or fear that makes you unable to think clearly or calmly'. What word is it?**

3 **Which word beginning with *m* describes the island? What does it mean?**

4 **Find a word in the story that begins with ...**

   a *st* and means 'walked and nearly fell over'.
   b *sh* and means 'shaking because you are cold or frightened'.
   c *sur* and means 'someone who is still alive'.

Language building

10

> The words that tell you **who is speaking** can come at the **beginning** or **end** of the sentence.
>
> 'Get out of my way. I want to get off this ship!' <u>the sailor screamed</u>.
>
> <u>The sailor screamed</u>, 'Get out of my way. I want to get off this ship!'
>
> Sometimes the words that tell you **who is speaking** can come in the **middle**.
>
> 'Get out of my way,' <u>the sailor screamed</u>. 'I want to get off this ship!'
>
> Notice that all the words the sailor said are **always** inside **speech marks**.

1 **Read these sentences. Discuss where the missing speech marks go.**

1 Give me my telescope. I want to see where we are, the captain ordered. _____

2 The sailor asked, Are we near the island? Can you see it yet? _____

3 Do you know this island? I asked. Do you know where the river is? _____

4 It's getting windy. I think a storm is coming, the sailor said. _____

5 The ship is sinking! the captain shouted. Jump into the sea! _____

6 I can't swim any more. I'm too tired, Jim said. _____

7 The boy said, I'm a good swimmer. I can swim a long way. _____

8 I'm hungry, I said. I want some food. _____

2 **Read the sentences again. Underline the words that tell you who is speaking. Write B (beginning), M (middle) or E (end) next to each sentence.**

3 **Discuss two other ways of writing each sentence.**

Grammar

Do you remember the story about the shipwreck?

The ship is sinking.

There aren't any lifeboats.

I can't swim.

The storm roared around them. Huge waves lifted the ship and threw it onto the rocks.

The captain shouted that the ship was sinking. A sailor said that there were not any lifeboats. A woman said that she could not swim.

1 Write the speech bubbles.

1 Jim said that he was tired.

2 A sailor said that the sea was cold.

3 A man said that the rocks were dangerous.

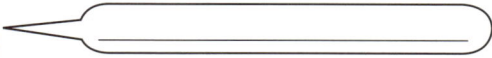

2 Put the verbs in the correct tense.

1 'I can see land!' The captain said that he _____ see land.
2 'The rocks are sharp!' A sailor said that the rocks _____ sharp.
3 'The wind is growing stronger.' A man said that the wind _____ stronger.

3 Ask and answer with a friend.

I can reach the island.

What did Jim say?

He said that he could reach the island.

I'm scared.

The waves are huge.

I can't jump.

The boat is going down.

Turn to Fluency Book 5 Programme 10.

Grammar   *reported speech – present tense becomes past tense*

Spelling

Say the words **shining** and **broken**.

Each of these words has got **two syllables**.

The **first** syllable of each word **contains** a **long vowel** (a vowel which says its name).

shi + ning = shining

bro + ken = broken

The sun is shining.

The wood is broken.

1 Put the syllables together. Write the word. Say the word.

1 ti + ger = _____

2 o + pen = _____

3 E + gypt = _____

4 ba + by = _____

5 stu + dent = _____

6 qui + et = _____

7 spi + der = _____

8 A + pril = _____

9 la + bel = _____

10 pa + per = _____

2 Choose the correct word to complete each sentence.

1 A _____ has got eight legs.

2 A _____ is not very old.

3 You write on _____ .

4 The book was _____ .

5 The teacher told the noisy children to be _____ .

6 _____ is the name of the month after March.

7 A _____ goes to school.

8 _____ is the name of a country.

9 My name was on the _____ on the present.

10 A _____ is a wild animal.

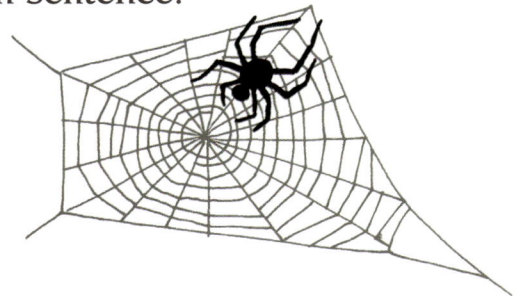

Class writing

Look at the map of the island on page 85. In Chapter 4 of 'The Shipwreck', Jim explored the island.

Don't spend a long time on this!

1 Discuss each of the places that are named on the map. Talk about what you think each place looks like.

2 Have a class vote. Choose the place you think Jim explored first.

3 Discuss:

Don't spend a long time on this, either!

- How did Jim get to the place?
- What did he take with him?
- Did anything happen on the way?
- What did Jim see when he reached the place?
- What did he think?
- How did he feel?

4 Write the first paragraph of Chapter 4 together on the board.

5 Discuss some things that could happen to Jim at the place and some things that could go wrong.

6 Choose one of these things that went wrong. Now write the second paragraph of Chapter 4 together on the board.

7 Discuss:

- How did Jim overcome the problem?
- What did he do? What did he think? How did he feel?
- What happened at the end? Was he hurt? Did he escape?

8 Write the last paragraph of Chapter 4 together on the board.

Now think of a good title for Chapter 4!

Reading for enrichment

The Dolphin

On a beach in the morning
The sea green and blue
A young child was resting:
The same age as you

From a spot near a towel
A whispering came
Like a rustle of leaves
Or a voice in a dream.

Where the ripples were circling
A dolphin appeared
And said 'Come down with me.'
And then – DISappeared.

The child entered softly
And reached the sea-floor
And saw not a sign
Of the golden sea-shore

There were molluscs in sea-shells
Anenomes too,
And more fish than the child
Had observed in the zoo.

On the back of the dolphin
The child wished and watched
How the fish gather round
As the fish-eggs are hatched.

Faster and faster
The dolphin progressed
And they passed near to China
As they streaked from the West.

And there were goldfish
As large as your knee,
And twenty-five pandas
Asleep by the sea.

In India fish had
The most wonderful marks
(But they missed out Australia
Because of the sharks).

At the end of the journey
They were back near the beach
When they talked of their trip
With bubbles for speech.

Then the child swam back strongly
To the spot on the sand
And covered up eyes
With the back of a hand.

In an hour the child woke up
In bed, it would seem.
Do you think that it happened
Or was it a dream?

Alan Bold

Exploring Greece

In geography, Ben's class was exploring different countries of the world. The teacher asked each child to pick a country and write a report on it. Ben chose Greece. First, he got an information book on Greece. Then he made some notes. He wrote his notes under different headings. Here are the notes he made.

Introduction
- Location — South East Europe, in the Mediterranean Sea
- Size — over 130,000 square kilometres
- Population — over 10 million
- Main language — Greek
- Capital city — Athens

Landscape
long coastline, 20% of country – small islands
plains and forest in the south; lots of mountains in north
highest mountain – Mount Olympus (2,917 metres high)
largest island – The island of Crete
longest river – The River Aliakmon (297 km long)

Main industries
tourism (historic sites; good beaches)
farming
fishing

History
ancient Greek civilisation – about 4,000 years old
historic sites to visit include:
The Parthenon in Athens
The Palace of Knossos in Crete (according to legend – the home of the Minotaur monster)

Stimulus summary notes/non-fiction report

Here is the report Ben wrote from his notes.

Introduction

Greece is in South East Europe and covers over 130,000 square kilometres. It is in the Mediterranean Sea. Greece has a population of over ten million people and its main language is Greek. Its capital city is Athens.

Landscape

Greece has got a long coastline. About twenty per cent of the country is made up of islands. The largest island is Crete. In the south of Greece there are plains and forests but in the north it is very mountainous. The highest mountain is Mount Olympus (2,917 metres high) and the longest river is Aliakmon (297 kilometres long).

Industries

The sea is important to Greece. Fishing is one of its main industries. Tourism is also an important industry because many people go to Greece for their holidays and there are many interesting historic places to visit. Farming is important, too.

History

Greece has a long history. The Ancient Greek civilisation began about 4,000 years ago. The Parthenon in Athens was built about 2,500 years ago and was a meeting place for the important people of the city. According to legend, a monster called the Minotaur was kept in a maze under the Palace of Knossos in Crete.

Comprehension

1 What is wrong with each sentence?
Correct these sentences. Write in your copy book.

1 Ben wrote a story about Greece.
2 Greece is in North East Europe.
3 The capital city of Greece is Rome.
4 Greece has not got a coastline.
5 About twenty per cent of the country is made up of big islands.
6 There are lots of mountains in the south of Greece.
7 The main industries are farming, fishing and fashion.
8 The Ancient Greek civilisation began about 2,500 years ago.

2 Discuss your answers to these questions.

1 Is a report fiction or non-fiction?
2 Why did Ben begin by writing some notes?
3 Are Ben's notes proper sentences?
4 Why did Ben write his notes and report under different headings?
5 How do the headings help you when you are reading?
6 Was Ben's report   a clear?
                                 b easy to read?
7 What was the most interesting thing you found out?

Vocabulary

Sometimes we have to look at a text very carefully.

1 Find a word on page 92 that contains the word:

a port   b head   c pop   d land

2 Match each word you found to its meaning.

1 titles at the top of pages or paragraphs   _____
2 how the land looks   _____
3 the number of people who live in a place   _____
4 a written description of a subject   _____

11

Language building

We can write a **sentence** as:

The Acropolis was built about 2,500 years ago.

a **statement**

When was it built?

a **question**

Look at that wonderful building!

an **exclamation**

A **statement** gives information.
When we write a statement we end it with a **full stop**.

When we want to know something we ask a **question**.
When we write a question we end it with a **question mark**.

An **exclamation** is when someone feels strongly about something.
It can show surprise, humour or give a warning.
When we write an exclamation we end it with an **exclamation mark**.

1 The words in these statements are in the wrong order.
Write the statements correctly.

1   capital is Greece the Athens of city

_____

Remember! Put a **full stop** at the end of each statement.

2   got Greece coastline has long a

_____

3   is island the Crete largest Greek

_____

4   Mount the is highest Olympus mountain

_____

2 Make up five questions about Greece for a friend to answer.
Write them down.

3 Fill in the missing *exclamation mark* at the end of each sentence below.
Read each exclamation with expression.
Discuss who you think said each thing and who you think they said it to.

Stop shouting at once

Look at my lovely photo

That's horrible

Grammar

What do you know about Athens?

The Parthenon **was built** about 2,500 years ago. It **was constructed** on a hill above the city. It **was made** from white marble. It **was used** as a meeting place.

This stadium **was built** a little later than the Parthenon. It **was used** for sports by the Ancient Greeks. It **was rebuilt** in 1869 and the first modern Olympic Games **were held** there in 1896. It **was used** again in the 2004 Olympics.

1 **Read and make sentences.**

1	The Parthenon was built	a	for sports.
2	It was made	b	at this stadium in 1896.
3	The old stadium was used	c	from white marble.
4	The first modern Olympic Games were held	d	on a hill above Athens.

2 **Complete these sentences. Use the words in the boxes.**

| was   were |

| called   used   held   built   constructed   kept |

1   The Palace of Knossos _____ _____ on the island of Crete. A monster _____ _____ in a maze under the palace. This monster _____ _____ the Minotaur.

2   The Olympic Games _____ _____ in Athens in 2004. A huge new Olympic Stadium _____ _____ for the Games but the old stadium _____ _____ for some events.

3 **Ask and answer. Use the words in the box.**

the Egyptians	the Aztecs
the French	the Chinese
the Greeks	the Romans

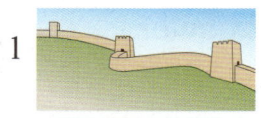

1   Who built this?

It was built by …

2   Who built these?

They were built by …

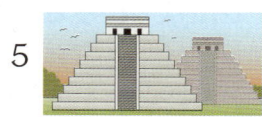

3   4   5   6

Grammar   *past simple passive*

Turn to Fluency Book 5 Programme 11.

Spelling

In some words the letters **ci** and **ti** sound like **sh**.
Say the sentence. Listen for the **sh** sounds.

The location of this ancient Greek building is Athens.

1 Make the words. Write the words. Say the words.

ci

spe _ci_ al   an___ent   deli___ous   musi___an   pre___ous

special   _____   _____   _____   _____

ti

loca___on   pa___ent   ini___al   popula___on   cau___ous

_____   _____   _____   _____   _____

2 Choose the correct word from Activity 1 to complete these sentences.

1   A _____ is someone who plays music.
2   Greece has a _____ of over ten million people.
3   Something that is very old is _____.
4   Another word for 'careful' is _____.
5   Gold is a _____ metal.
6   The _____ letter of 'location' is 'l'.
7   I ate all the pizza. It was _____.
8   The _____ of the treasure is a secret.
9   Amy is my best friend. She is very _____.
10 When you wait for a long time you have to be very _____.

Class writing

Finish these notes I wrote about **Italy**. Use the notes on page 92 to help you.

1 **Complete the missing words.**

I_____   L_____   South Europe
                S_____   over 300,000 square _____
                P_____   over 57 million
                M_____I_____   Italian
                C_____c_____   Rome

L_____   long thin country, the shape of a boot!
                long coastline
                mountains and lakes in north
                in the south: plains and smaller mountains
                highest m _____ – Mont Blanc (4,807 metres high)
                two large islands to south – Sicily and Sardinia
                longest r _____– The River Po (652 km long)

M_____I_____   tourism;    farming;

                vehicles;    electronics;

                fashion

H_____   ancient Roman c _____ – about 2,500 years old
                historic s _____to visit include:
                The Colosseum in Rome
                Pompeii (where Mount Vesuvius
                erupted in the first century)

2 **Now use these notes and write a report about Italy together on the board.**

Use the report on page 93 to help you.
Write four paragraphs of information.
Don't forget to give each paragraph a heading.
Find or draw some pictures to go with your report.

Reading for enrichment

Marco Polo – a famous explorer

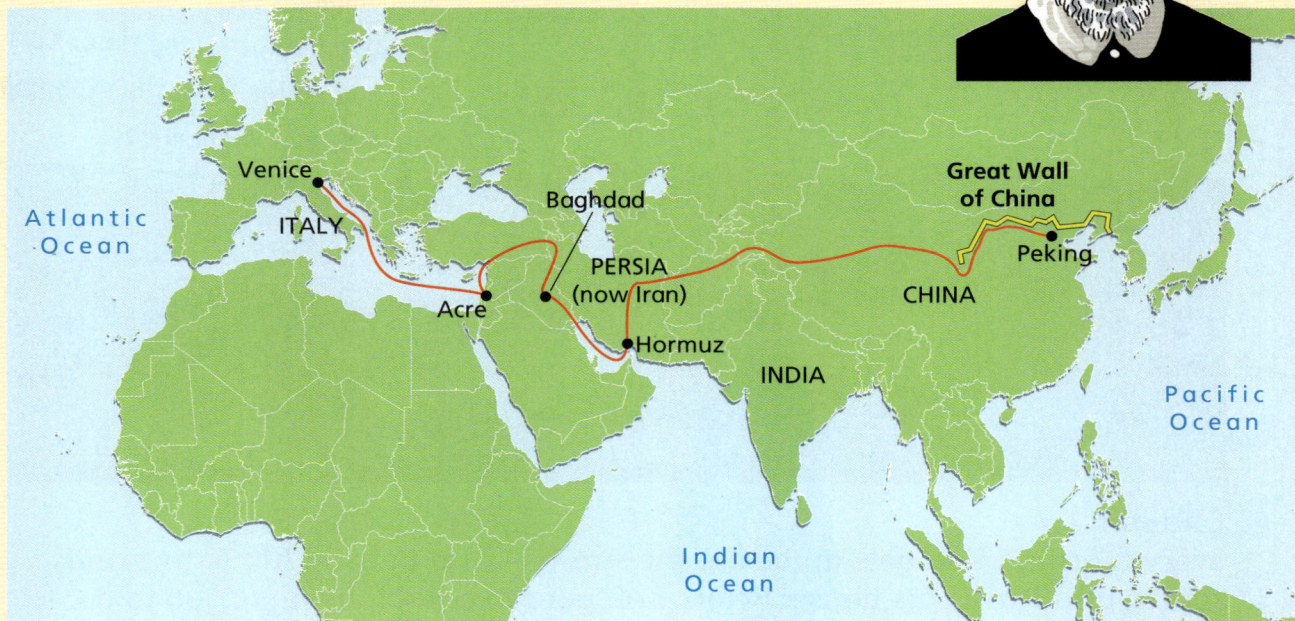

Marco Polo was born about 1254 in Venice in Italy. Marco's father was a merchant. Marco learnt about travelling and exploring from his father.

In the year Marco was born, his father and his uncle set out on a long journey to China. At that time, no-one knew much about China. They reached Peking (the city that is now called Beijing) and were welcomed by the Emperor. The Chinese people were amazed to see them. Marco's father and his uncle were the first people from Europe to visit China.

They stayed in China for fifteen years and saw many wonderful things. When they returned to Italy they brought lots of Chinese things, like silk materials and spices, to sell. They told Marco exciting stories about their travels and about all the amazing things they had seen in China.

When Marco was 17 he left Italy with his father and uncle. They went to China by a different route. They had lots of adventures on the way. It took them four years to get there. The Emperor liked Marco and gave him a job in his government. Marco stayed in China for 24 years.

Then Marco decided to return to Venice. When he arrived home, he wrote about his travels and his adventures. He wrote about the Chinese people and their customs. He wrote about how kind and clever they were. Many people learned about China from Marco Polo.

The Stream

Kofi lives with his family in a small village in the centre of Africa. A river runs through the village. The river became polluted a few years ago. The villagers have taken water from a standpipe for a long time. Kofi has fetched water from the standpipe since he was a small boy.

Chapter 1

Every morning Kofi gets up before the sun rises. He puts on his T-shirt and shorts, and leaves his house. Before Kofi goes to school, he has a job to do. He makes a trip to the standpipe to get clean water for his family. Every morning, Kofi and his friends go to fetch water in metal drums, plastic buckets, and all sorts of other containers. Every family sends someone for water.

The village is always a lively place early in the morning. Kofi meets his school friends and they all set out together. They tell each other jokes and stories along the way. It is a long walk to the standpipe and seems even longer coming back. Sometimes Kofi is lucky enough to get a ride on a cart or truck passing by.

Once a stream of clear, clean water ran down from the forest to the village. The stream gave the village good fresh water. Then suddenly the stream became polluted. The water had a bad smell and the villagers could not drink it any more.

One day Kofi was struggling back to the village with two heavy plastic containers of water when he heard a donkey cart coming. It was Old Man Awam, the tanner. Awam's job was to turn animal skins into leather. His tannery was up in the forest above the village. He did not often come down to the village. When he did, he always seemed to be in a bad temper.

There were lots of old oil drums on Awam's cart. Kofi looked at the drums and thought that Awam must use a lot of water at his tannery. The boy waved to the old man. Kofi hoped that Awam would stop and give him a ride. But Awam frowned and drove on. Kofi was left in a cloud of dust.

Chapter 2

It was an important day for Kofi but he was exhausted. In the morning he fetched the water as usual. All day he and his friends had practised hard for their school play that evening. Then Mrs Awooner, their teacher, sent the children to invite people who lived outside the village to the play. She asked Kofi to go and invite Old Man Awam. Everybody knew he did not like children.

Kofi walked slowly up the steep hill behind the village towards the rainforest. Kofi tried to think of his part in the play as he climbed the path through the gloomy forest. The closer he got to Awam's house, the more nervous he became. He remembered how bad-tempered Old Man Awam was when they last met. Also something else made Kofi nervous. There was a horrible smell drifting through the forest. It was the smell of animal skins drying in the sun. Kofi knew it was Awam's job to make leather. He understood why Awam's tannery was a long way from the village. The smell was awful! He also understood why people did not go near the place. But Kofi thought there was something familiar about the nasty smell.

Then Kofi saw somebody moving through the bushes towards him. It was Awam. The old man was mumbling to himself as he rolled a heavy oil drum in front of him. Kofi thought it contained water. 'I wonder why Awam is taking water through the forest? I will hide behind a bush and see what he is going to do,' Kofi said to himself. Kofi hid behind a bush and watched. He could see Awam's house. Outside it there were many other oil drums. They were like the ones Kofi saw on Awam's cart. Kofi decided to follow the old man to find out.

Kofi followed Awam to the stream. Awam stopped and looked around. Then he frowned and looked straight towards the bush where Kofi was hiding. For a moment Kofi thought the old man looked straight at him. Kofi held his breath.

After a moment, Awam bent down and pulled the lid off the drum. Kofi watched him. He poured a dirty yellow liquid into the stream. At first Kofi thought it was just dirty water. After a few moments a terrible smell drifted towards him. 'Where have I smelled that smell before?' whispered Kofi to himself. Then he remembered. It was the smell that came from the village stream. The mystery of the village stream was solved. It was Awam who was polluting it!

Comprehension

1 **Complete the text with the correct words. Discuss your answers.**

Every morning Kofi and his friends went from their village to the standpipe to get clean (1) _____ . It was a (2) _____ way to the standpipe. One day Kofi was going home with two containers of water. He saw Old Man Awam on a donkey (3) _____ . He was a (4) _____ . His tannery was up in the forest above the village. Kofi waved but the old man did not (5) _____ .
In the evening Mrs Awooner, Kofi's teacher, sent him to (6) _____ Old Man Awam to their school play. When Kofi got near the tannery there was an (7) _____ smell. Kofi saw Old Man Awam moving through the (8) _____ towards him. The old man was rolling a (9) _____ oil drum in front of him. Kofi (10) _____ the old man to the stream. Awam pulled the lid off the oil drum and (11) _____ a dirty yellow (12) _____ into the stream.

2 **Discuss your answers to these questions.**

1 How do you know that Kofi liked to fetch water from the standpipe?
2 Why did it seem a long way coming back from the standpipe?
3 How did Kofi feel when Old Man Awam did not stop and give him a ride?
4 Why did Kofi walk slowly up the hill towards the rainforest?
5 Why was the tannery a long way from the village?
6 Do you like Old Man Awam? Give your reasons.

Vocabulary

Words with similar meanings are called **synonyms**.

1 **Find each word below in the story on pages 100 and 101.**
Match the words with their synonyms. Use the thesaurus on page 166.

1 polluted	_c_	a glared	5 bad-tempered	____	e muttering
2 fetch	____	b fighting	6 gloomy	____	f fluid
3 frowned	____	c unclean	7 mumbling	____	g dark
4 struggling	____	d bring	8 liquid	____	h irritable

2 **Now make up some sentences of your own. Use these words in them.**

Language building

12

> First I hid behind a rock.

> Now I am hiding behind a tree.

> Next I will hide behind that bush.

This happened in the **past**. The verb is in the **past tense**.

This is happening **now**. It is in the **present tense**.

This will happen in the **future**. It is in the **future tense**.

1   **Complete this table correctly.**

verb	past tense	present tense	future tense
to wash	I washed.	I am __washing__.	I will __wash__.
to walk	You walked.	You are _____.	You will _____.
to run	He ran.	He is _____.	He will _____.
to leave	She left.	She is _____.	She will _____.
to eat	It ate.	It is _____.	It will _____.
to smile	We smiled.	We are _____.	We will _____.
to hide	They hid.	They are _____.	They will _____.

2   **Underline the verbs in these sentences.**

1   Kofi woke up early.
2   He washed his face.
3   He dressed in his T-shirt and shorts.
4   Kofi ate his breakfast.
5   Then he picked up a plastic container.
6   He left his house.
7   He met his friends in the village square.
8   Then they all walked to the standpipe.
9   They collected clean water in their containers.
10   Kofi and his friends returned to the village with the water.

> They are all in the **past tense**.

3   **Discuss how to change each sentence above into the *future tense*. Write each sentence and underline the *verb* in it.**

1   Kofi will wake up early.

Grammar

Who lives in Sam's village?

These are some of the people in my village.

Mrs Kay is my teacher. She has been at the village school since last spring.

Mr Bell is our baker. His father and his grandfather were bakers in the village, too. His family has lived here for years and years.

Mr Archer is a farmer. His family have been on their farm since 1999.

Mr Hobbs is the blacksmith. He moved to the village last month but he has worked as a blacksmith for twenty-five years.

1 **Circle true (T) or false (F).**

1	The Bells have lived in the village for a short time.	T	F
2	Mrs Kay has taught at the village school since last autumn.	T	F
3	Mr Hobbs has been a blacksmith for a long time.	T	F
4	Mr Hobbs has lived in the village for a long time.	T	F
5	Mr Archer has worked on his farm since 2003.	T	F

2 **Correct the false sentences. Say then write.**

3 **Answer these questions. Use the words in the boxes.**

for a long time for a short time	since 1999 since last month since last spring

1 How long have the Archers been on their farm?
2 How long has Mr Hobbs worked as a blacksmith?
3 How long has Mrs Kay taught at the village school?
4 How long have the Bells baked bread in the village?
5 How long has Mr Hobbs lived in the village?

4 **Answer these questions. Then ask and answer with a friend.**

Turn to Fluency Book 5 Programme 12.

1 How long have you lived in this town? _____
2 How long have you been at this school? _____
3 How long have you known your best friend? _____

Spelling

Sometimes **different letter patterns** can make the **same sound**.
Read the words below. The **ea** and **ee** make the same sound.

a str**ea**m

a st**ee**p hill

1 Look back at the story. Find these words.
Read the words in each set.

What do you notice about the sound of the letter patterns in bold in each set?

set 1	str**ea**m	st**ee**p	
set 2	d**ow**n	cl**ou**d	
set 3	sch**oo**l	kn**ew**	
set 4	pl**ay**	cont**ai**ners	
set 5	n**er**vous	t**ur**n	T-sh**ir**t
set 6	sh**or**ts	exh**au**sted	**aw**ful

2 Discuss the meaning of each word.

3 What new word can you make if you:

1 change the **str** in **str**eam to **dr**?   _dream_

2 change the **st** in **st**eep to **d**?   _____

3 change the **d** in **d**own to **t**?   _____

4 change the **cl** in **cl**oud to **l**?   _____

5 change the **sch** in **sch**ool to **p**?   _____

6 change the **kn** in **kn**ew to **dr**?   _____

7 change the **pl** in **pl**ay to **aw**?   _____

8 change the **t** in **t**urn to **b**?   _____

9 change the **sh** in **sh**irt to **sk**?   _____

10 change the **sh** in **sh**orts to **sp**?   _____

Class writing

All stories have a **setting** (where they take place). Look at the picture of the village early in the morning.

- Where is the village?
- What time of day is it?

Discuss these questions. Then write a class description of the village.

1 Imagine what you can see.

- What is the village like?
- How are the houses made?
- What is coming out of some roofs? Why?
- Who are gathering in the village centre? How are they dressed?
- What are they carrying? Why?
- How will they get to the standpipe?

2 Imagine what sounds you can hear.

Can you hear any noise from:
a the children?   b the houses?   c the river?   d any animals?

3 Imagine what you can smell.

Reading for enrichment

How to make a solar still

If you are nowhere near a source of water you can survive by making a solar still.

What you need

a spade   a plastic or polythene sheet   some heavy stones   a clean container

What you do:

Step 1 Dig a hole about a metre deep and about a metre across the top.

Step 2 Place the container in the centre of the hole.

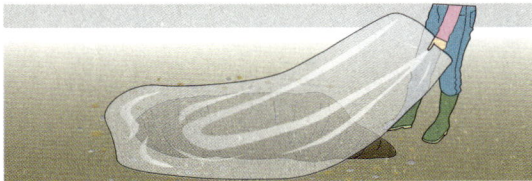

Step 3 Stretch the polythene or plastic sheet across the top of the hole.

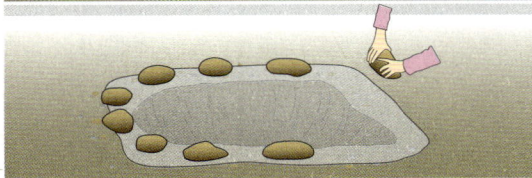

Step 4 Place the stones around the edge of the hole to hold the sheet in place.

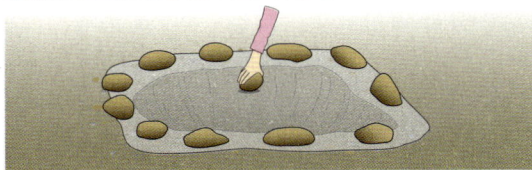

Step 5 Place a heavy stone carefully in the centre of the sheet, above the container.

How the solar still works

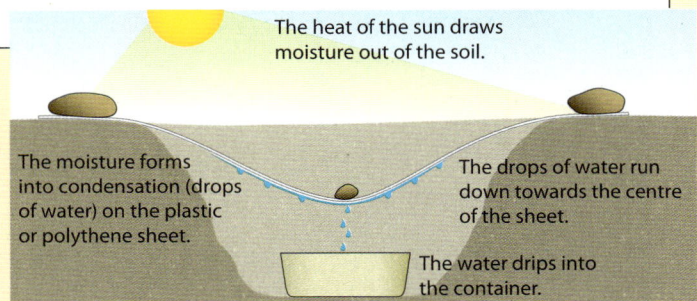

The heat of the sun draws moisture out of the soil.

The moisture forms into condensation (drops of water) on the plastic or polythene sheet.

The drops of water run down towards the centre of the sheet.

The water drips into the container.

Join World Watch

LOOK FORWARD TO A BETTER FUTURE WITH WORLD WATCH!

What are the problems?

- Our forests are **disappearing**.
- Our air and water are **unclean**.
- Many animals are becoming **extinct**.
- There is **pollution** everywhere.

What is the answer?

Join World Watch!
World Watch has been working for 30 years to make the world a **better** place.

With your help, we have:

- **asked** governments to pass laws about pollution
- **encouraged** people to recycle materials
- **stopped** some factories polluting the atmosphere
- **prevented** oil spills at sea
- **protected** the world's wildlife
- **reduced** traffic pollution in our cities

Join World Watch

What sort of world do you want to grow up in?
You can help change the world.
You can make a difference!

When you join World Watch you will receive ...

- an information pack about our work
- a leaflet to give to a friend
- a 'Save the World' poster
- a 'World Watch Watch' – to remind you that every second counts
- regular information on new projects
- a monthly World Watch magazine – full of interesting information and advice, photographs, a puzzle page, competitions and much, much more.

Our promise

WE PROMISE WE WILL SPEND EVERY PENNY YOU GIVE TO MAKE THE WORLD A BETTER PLACE

Comprehension

1 **Say** *true*, *false* **or** *can't tell.*

1 The leaflet was written by World Watch.
2 Our water and air are getting cleaner.
3 The worst problem is pollution from cars.
4 World Watch is more than 25 years old.
5 World Watch has stopped every factory polluting the atmosphere.
6 World Watch has encouraged people to ride bicycles.
7 World Watch has protected whales and dolphins.

2 **Discuss your answers to these questions.**

1 What does 'People use words to persuade us to do things.' mean?
2 Number the problems 1–4 in order of importance.
3 Look at the 'With your help …' part of the leaflet. What do you think is the biggest success of World Watch?
4 What do you think is the best thing you will receive when you join World Watch?
5 Explain why you think the leaflet is good or not.
6 How can we all help to make the world 'a better place'?

Vocabulary

> Underline the word in each set that comes from the leaflet on pages 108 and 109.

1 **Write each set of words in alphabetical order.**

1 leopard	leaflet	lemonade	letter
2 recycle	rescue	release	record
3 advance	admit	advice	admire
4 enjoyed	entered	enclosed	encouraged
5 prefix	prevented	pretended	prepared

Language building

(subject)	(verb)	(object)		(object)	(verb)	(subject)
The man	**read**	a leaflet.		A leaflet	**was read**	by the man.

The verb is **active**.
The subject (the man)
did something (read)
to something (a leaflet).

The verb is **passive**.
The object (a leaflet)
 has something done to it (was read)
 by the subject (the man).

> The verbs in these sentences are all **active** verbs.

1 **Discuss which is the subject (S), verb (V) and object (O) in each sentence.**

       (S)   (V)   (O)

1 The lady drove the silver car.
2 The bad man shot the elephant.
3 The farmer cleared the forest.
4 Kofi collected some clean water.
5 The factory polluted the atmosphere.
6 The children recycled some glass bottles.
7 The ship spilt some oil.
8 Tom received a World Watch magazine.

> The verbs in these sentences are all **passive** verbs.

2 **Discuss which is the subject (S), verb (V) and object (O) in each sentence. Then match the active sentences in 1 with the passive sentences in 2.**

       (S)   (V)   (O)

a Some oil was spilt by the ship.   7
b The silver car was driven by the lady.   ____
c The atmosphere was polluted by the factory.   ____
d A World Watch magazine was received by Tom.   ____
e Some clean water was collected by Kofi.   ____
f The elephant was shot by the bad man.   ____
g Some glass bottles were recycled by the children.   ____
h The forest was cleared by the farmer.   ____

Grammar

What do you remember about World Watch?

World Watch has been working for thirty years to make the world a better place.

Jenny Cook works for World Watch. She has been living in Borneo since 1995. For over ten years she has been working in the rainforest. She has been studying orang-utans, a kind of monkey.

'The orang-utans are in danger,' says Jenny. 'For years people have been cutting down the trees. The orang-utans need the forest. It is their home. If there are fewer trees, there are fewer orang-utans.'

1 Correct these sentences.

1 Jenny Cook has been living in Borneo since 1990.
2 She has been working on a farm.
3 She has been painting orang-utans.
4 People have been cutting down trees for six months.
5 The forests have been getting bigger.
6 The number of orang-utans has been rising.

2 Complete these sentences with the words in the boxes.

has been have been	increasing disappearing getting polluting

1 In recent years rainforests _____ _____ .
2 That factory _____ _____ the air since it was built.
3 For years traffic _____ _____ in our cities.
4 Pollution _____ _____ worse for many years.

3 Answer these questions. Then ask and answer with a friend.

1 How long have you been studying English? _____
2 How long have we been using this book? _____
3 How long have we been sitting in this classroom? _____

Turn to Fluency Book 5 Programme 13.

Spelling

A **suffix** is a group of letters that we add to the **end** of a word.

Notice that there is only **one l** in the suffix **ful**.

When we add the suffix **less** the word means the **opposite**.

power + ful = power**ful**
(powerful means 'full of power')

power + less = power**less**
(powerless means 'has no power')

1 Add the suffix *ful* to each word. Write the word.

1 power ful
   powerful

2 care _____
   _____

3 use _____
   _____

4 pain _____
   _____

5 help _____
   _____

6 colour _____
   _____

2 Which word means the opposite of these words?

1 useful _____
3 colourful _____

2 powerful _____
4 painful _____

3 Discuss each sentence. Choose the correct word to complete it.

1 The TV was broken. It was _____ (useful/useless).
2 The painting was bright and _____ (colourful/colourless).
3 The boy's writing was untidy and _____ (careful/careless).
4 I hurt my leg. It was very _____ (painful/painless).
5 The strong man was very _____ (powerful/powerless).
6 It is good to be _____ (helpful/helpless) at home.

Class writing

There has been a terrible disaster in another country. World Watch want to make a poster to persuade people to help.

- Brainstorm your ideas.
- Write them on the board.
- Choose the best ideas.
- Then finish the poster!

1. **Decide what sort of disaster you think it was.**
   - floods
   - famine
   - earthquake
   - something else

2. **Think of some short facts to go in each star below.**

3. **Think of another picture for the poster below.**

4. **Think of another rhyme to complete the speech bubble below.**

World Watch needs your help NOW!

Terrible disaster!

Children starving!

Give your money. Please **donate**. Do it now – it's not too **late**!

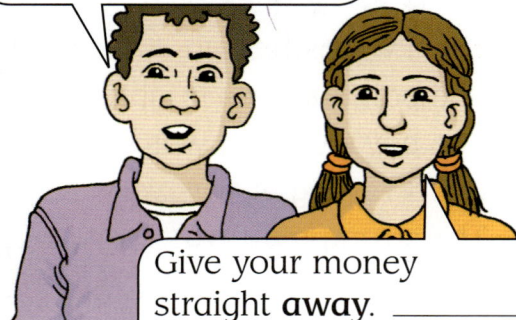

Give your money straight **away**. _____

Reading for enrichment

The litter song 🎧

Chorus
Litter, litter, everywhere.
Litter, litter, do we care?
The world is full of rubbish.
It really is a mess.
We must clean it up
So it will look its best.

Verse 1
There's litter on the pavement
And there's litter on the street.
There's litter almost everywhere
You want to put your feet.
There's litter in the park,
Oh, what are we to do?
If someone's going to clear it up,
It's up to me and you.

Chorus

Verse 2
So if you have a wrapper,
Or an empty cola tin,
Just put it in your pocket
Till you find a bin.
Try to keep things tidy,
Don't put things on the floor,
We don't want any litter,
We don't want it any more.

Chorus

Andrew Jackson

Revision 3

1 **Have you ever seen an ancient building?**
What was it?
Where was it?
Have you been to a museum?
What did you see there?

2 **Listen and read.** 🎧

3 **Read and answer.**
Look at picture a.
1 How old is the theatre?
2 Who performed the plays?
3 How many people watched the plays?
4 What kind of plays did they see?

Look at picture b.
1 When were the Olympic Games held in Athens?
2 How old are the modern Olympics?
3 Why was the new stadium built?

Look at picture c.
1 What were Greek ships made of?
2 Who told stories about them?
3 How long has the professor worked in the museum?

This theatre is very old. It was built 3000 years ago. Actors performed plays here and thousands of people came to watch. Some plays were funny and some were sad.

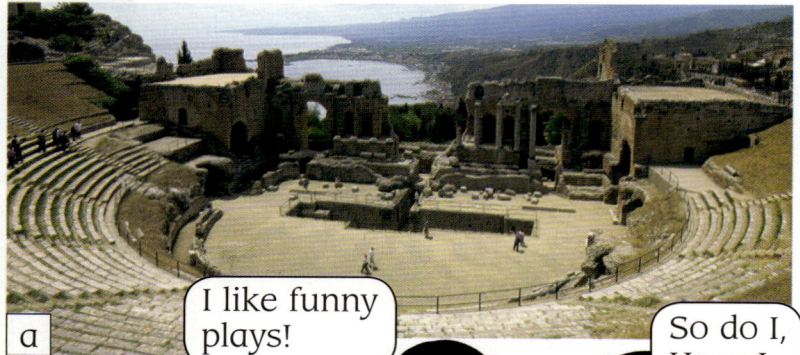

a

I like funny plays!

So do I, Harry!

The Greeks built huge wooden ships and had many adventures at sea. Greek poets told stories about them and artists painted pictures of them.

c

This is the most interesting museum in the world!

He has worked in this museum for 50 years!

Athletes have been competing in the modern Olympics since 1896. The 2004 Olympic games were held in Athens. This new stadium was built for the games.

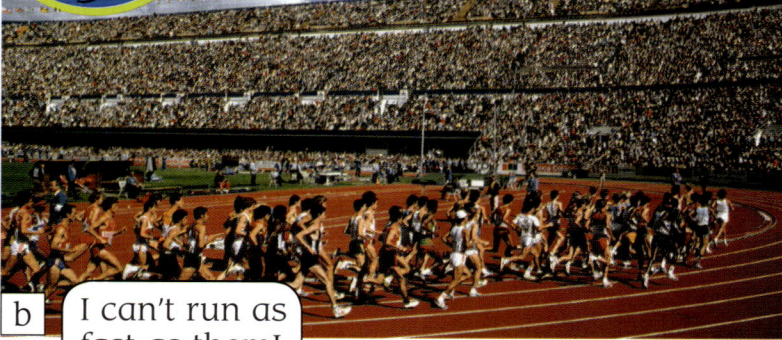

b

I can't run as fast as them!

Neither can I, Baz!

Tourists have been visiting the Acropolis for hundreds of years. It is the most famous place in Athens. Hundreds of pictures of it are bought every year.

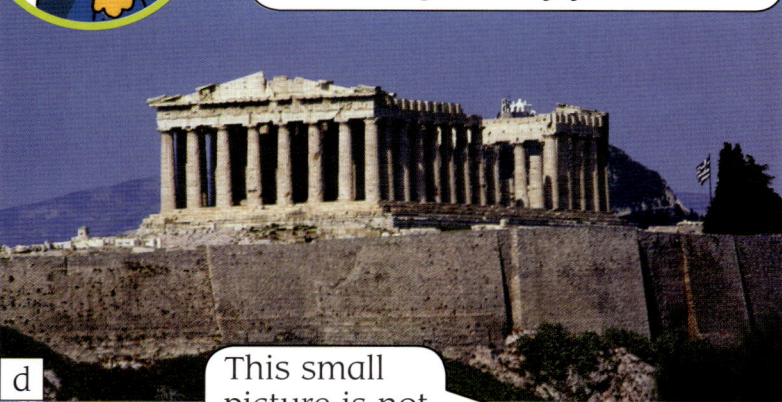

d

This small picture is not expensive.

Look at picture d.

1 What is the most famous place in Athens?
2 Who visits it?
3 What do they buy?

4 What did they say?

She said the theatre was very old.

1    2

3    4

5 Listen and say which place.

1 ___   2 ___   3 ___   4 ___

Which things did Harry take a picture of?

the vase ☐   the theatre ☐
Acropolis ☐   the runners ☐

6 Write sentences.
Plays/perform/actors.

Plays were performed by actors.

1 The play/watch/people.
2 Races/run/athletes.
3 Ships/build/Greeks.
4 Stories/tell/poets.
5 Pictures/paint/artists.

117

Kate is made smaller

Kate saw that her brother James was working on a fantastic machine.

'What's that?' she asked.

'It's a three-dimensional enlarger,' he said proudly.

'A what?' Kate asked.

'It makes things larger,' replied James.

'Is it like enlarging a photocopy?' asked Kate.

'Yes, but this machine doesn't just make a larger copy of something. It actually makes the thing itself bigger.'

Kate knew about three-dimensional things. 'Like this banana,' she said, picking it up. 'It's not just curved, and long. It's thick as well.'

James told Kate to put the banana in the machine. Then he switched on the light. Kate was amazed. It really worked! The real length of the banana was about 20 centimetres, but under the machine it grew to about 60 centimetres. She picked up the banana from the enlarger. It still kept its giant size.

'Wow! This is an important invention, isn't it?' she asked.

'Yes,' said James. 'My machine can also make things smaller. You just turn this handle the other way like this …'

James put a book under the light and turned the handle. The book became so small that the print was impossible to read.

'Wow! It's an ensmaller, too!' Kate laughed.

'Be careful,' James said. 'This machine is dangerous. If you put your hand in the machine, it would make it small, too.' Kate shuddered at the thought. James told Kate not to let anyone touch the machine.

But the next day, when Kate's friend Sara came to play, Kate showed her the machine while James was downstairs. She was explaining how it worked when Sara turned the handle. Immediately, Kate disappeared. Sara was puzzled. 'Where has she gone?' she wondered.

She ran downstairs to the kitchen. 'Have you seen Kate?' she asked Kate's Mum. James was walking past the kitchen and heard the conversation. He realised at once what was wrong. How could he tell his mother that Kate was now no bigger than an ant!

'I think she went that way,' he said to Sara, and pointed to the garden. James told Sara to look in the garden. She went off to find Kate and James ran upstairs and ran into his bedroom. Then he stopped. 'If I put my foot on her, I'll squash her,' he thought. 'Oh, what a terrible problem!'

He got down on his knees and started looking for his sister. Then he saw a little creature waving its arms about. It was Kate. She was looking at a spider's web. 'Kate!' shouted James. 'Come away from that web! A spider will be like a monster to you! Oh, Kate, I'm so sorry.' He picked her up gently.

'Sorry? For what?' squeaked Kate in excitement. She did not sound anxious, or afraid. 'It's wonderful, being so small!'

Comprehension

1 **Look back. Find the correct answers. Circle them.**

1 What was the name of James' sister?
    a Sara   b Anna   c Kate
2 What was James working on?
    a a drawing   b a machine   c a photocopier
3 What did James make larger?
    a a banana   b a hand   c a spider
4 What did James make smaller?
    a a handle   b an ant   c a book
5 Who came to play?
    a Kate   b Sara   c James
6 What was the 'tiny creature' looking at?
    a a spider's web   b a mouse   c an ant

2 **Discuss your answers to these questions.**

1 How do you know James was a clever boy?
2 Why was he proud of his machine?
3 Was it wrong of Kate to show Sara the machine?
4 Why didn't Sara know where Kate was?
5 How did James feel when he realised what was wrong?
6 Why wasn't Kate afraid of being so small?

Vocabulary

> Remember! A **noun** is a **naming** word.
> A **verb** is a **doing** word.
> An **adjective** is a **describing** word.

1 **Decide if each word is a noun (n), verb (v), or adjective (adj).**

1 machine   _n_   2 fantastic   ____   3 terrible   ____

4 realised   ____   5 anxious   ____   6 wonderful ____

7 conversation ____ 8 science   ____   9 shuddered ____

2 **Find each word in the story on pages 118 and 119.**
Discuss the meaning of each word.

Language building

Sometimes we talk about the **gender** of a noun.

James is a boy.

Kate is a girl.

Boy is a **masculine** (male) noun.

Girl is a **feminine** (female) noun.

1 Match the masculine and feminine nouns.

1 boy   _d_   a woman
2 man   ____   b wife
3 brother   ____   c niece
4 husband   ____   d girl
5 father   ____   e princess
6 uncle   ____   f queen
7 nephew   ____   g aunt
8 king   ____   h sister
9 prince   ____   i mother

2 What is the gender of each underlined noun?

1 Two <u>boys</u> were playing in the park. ____
2 The <u>friends</u>, Anna and Amy, went home together. ____
3 The <u>inventor</u> finished his fantastic new machine. ____
4 My <u>teacher</u>, Mrs Brown, is very nice. ____
5 The <u>lady</u> was shopping. ____
6 I like my <u>uncle</u> very much. ____
7 My <u>grandmother</u> is very kind to me. ____
8 The <u>police officer</u> got out of his car. ____

Grammar

Do you remember the story about James's invention?

James called Kate into his room. He *told* her *to sit down* and then he showed her his fantastic machine. He made a banana bigger and a book smaller. Amazing! Kate *asked* him *to do* it again.

Just then they heard their mother calling. She *told* them *to come* downstairs for dinner. Before they went downstairs, James *told* Kate *not to touch* the machine. He also *asked* her *not to tell* anyone about his invention.

1 Cover the text above.
Read these sentences. Circle the correct word.

1	James showed Kate his	a	computer.	b	invention.
2	He made a banana	a	bigger.	b	smaller.
3	Kate asked him to do it	a	again.	b	four more times.
4	James told Kate not to … the machine				
		a	take	b	touch
5	He also asked her … anyone about his invention.				
		a	to tell	b	not to tell

2 What did James tell Kate to do?

Come into my room!

He told her to come into his room.

1 Sit down!
3 Put the book in the machine!
2 Look at my invention!
4 Turn the handle!

3 What did James tell Kate not to do?

Don't touch the machine!

He told her not to touch the machine.

1 Don't shout!
3 Don't go near the spider!
2 Don't tell anyone!
4 Don't worry!

Turn to Fluency Book 5 Programme 14.

Grammar reported commands

Spelling

Sometimes **a** sounds like **o** (as in h<u>o</u>t) when it cames **after w**.

Kate w**a**s very small.

I w**a**nt that w**a**tch.

1   Say these words. Discuss what they mean.

w**a**sp	sw**a**n	w**a**tch	w**a**sh	w**a**llet	sw**a**llow

2   Match each word to the correct picture. Write the word.

1 _____   2 _____   3 _____

4 _____   5 _____   6 _____

3   The letters in these words are in the wrong order. Write the words.

1 tawn   <u>*want*</u>   2 aws   _____

3 wpas   _____   4 tawch   _____

5 shaw   _____   6 lawlet   _____

7 slowawl   _____   8 wnas   _____

Class writing

Use the ideas from 'Kate is made smaller' on pages 118 and 119 to write your own **story**. Begin your story like this:

James tried to make Kate bigger again – but the machine did not work!

'I'll mend the machine this afternoon,' he said. 'I must go downstairs for lunch now.'

He left Kate in the room and shut the door. Just then a spider appeared …

1 **Discuss your ideas.**
   Think about the questions below. Make some notes on the board.

- What did the spider look like to Kate?
- How did Kate feel?
- What did she think?
- What did the spider do?
- What did Kate do?
- Did the spider catch her? How?
- Did Kate escape? How?
- Did James return at any time?
- Did anything different happen?

2 **Write your story together on the board.**

When you have finished, read your story together and edit it.
Does it make sense?
Can you improve it in any way?
Do you want to:
- leave anything out?
- move any sentences to a different position?
- change any words to make them more exciting?
- add any more describing words?

Reading for enrichment

Cat's eyes

Percy Shaw was a very ordinary boy. He was born in 1890. He came from a large family of 14 children. His family were very poor. When he grew up, Percy mended roads.

One night, Percy was walking home in a fog. It was difficult to see. Suddenly Percy saw a car with its headlights on. It was going past him. Then he saw two bright spots of light ahead of the car. Percy realised that they were cat's eyes! The lights of the car reflected in the cat's eyes. This gave Percy an idea.

For months Percy thought about his idea. He spent hours in his shed experimenting with different things. Then he found the answer! He made some round pieces of glass and discovered that they reflected light from his torch when he shone it at them. When some of these pieces of glass were put along the centre of the road they reflected a car's headlights. This guided the car safely along the road. Percy discovered that his invention worked even in a fog.

By the time Percy died in 1976 his invention was used all over the world. Percy's tiny pieces of glass, his little cat's eyes, inside cases made of rubber, have made roads safer and have prevented many accidents.

Television

John Logie Baird was born in Scotland on 14th August, 1888. When he was a boy, he was never very clever at school. His school reports all said that he had to 'work harder' and that he 'could do better'.

Television is part of our everyday lives. It is difficult to imagine life without television. We can thank John Logie Baird for inventing television.

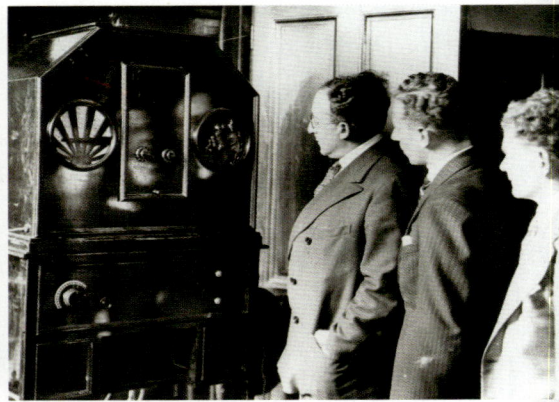

This did not worry John Logie Baird. He was always experimenting and inventing things. One day he connected his house to four of his friend's houses with electric wires. He wanted them to have their own telephone system. Unfortunately, one of the wires hung down too low and caused an accident. It made a driver of a coach crash.

Later John Logie Baird built a glider (a plane without an engine) and took it onto the roof of his house. He got in it. A friend had to push it off the roof to make it fly. The glider did not fly. It crashed down onto the ground! Luckily John Logie Baird was not hurt. He never liked flying after this!

John Logie Baird was always interested in engines and how things worked. He learned to be an electrician. Once he tried to make diamonds with electricity. He didn't succeed but he did blow up the electricity system of the whole town. No-one had any electricity that day!

John was always fascinated with the idea of sending moving pictures. He experimented for years. He failed many times but he did not give up. He was certain he could do it. Between 1924 and 1927 he succeeded. He sent moving pictures from one place to another. He even sent them across the Atlantic Ocean from Scotland to America. John had invented television. The age of television was here!

My teacher asked me to give my opinion of television. I made a list of the advantages and disavantages to help me plan my talk.

Advantages	Disadvantages
1 It helps you relax.	1 It can make you lazy.
2 It helps you with school work.	2 There's too much violence.
3 You can learn a lot about other countries.	3 Most of the programmes are terrible.
4 It offers you a choice – you can always find something that interests you.	4 It causes arguments – someone always wants to watch something different.
5 It entertains you.	5 It stops you from talking.
6 It stops you from getting into trouble.	6 You don't have time to play with your friends.

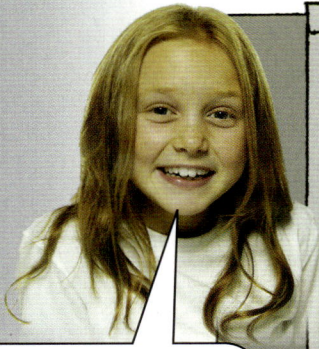

I wanted to give a positive opinion of television.
I picked three of the advantages.
I also wanted to be fair, so I picked one disadvantage.
Here is the talk I gave.

I think television is a good thing. I have several reasons to support my point of view.

My first reason is that television can help you with your school work. There are lots of educational programmes on TV. My second reason is that it helps you relax. After a hard day at school, and doing your homework, we all need to be able to relax for a while! Another reason why I think television is good is that it offers you a choice. You can always find something of interest to watch.

Some people do not agree. They think television is not good for you. They think it makes you lazy.

However, on the whole I believe that television is good if you think about what you watch, choose the programmes sensibly and don't watch too much.

Comprehension

1 **Answer these questions in your copy book.**

1 What did John Logie Baird's school reports say about him?
2 How did he make a coach crash?
3 How did John Logie Baird blow up the town's electricity system?
4 When did John Logie Baird succeed in inventing television?
5 How many advantages of television did the girl list?
6 On her list, what was   a the first advantage?
                                 b the last advantage?
7 How many disadvantages did she list?
8 On her list, what was   a the second disadvantage?
                                 b the fifth disadvantage?

2 **Discuss your answers to these questions.**

1 Why do you think John Logie Baird's teachers were surprised at his success when he left school?
2 Why do you think John tried to make diamonds?
3 Was John a patient man? Did he give up easily when things went wrong?
4 How did he feel when he succeeded in inventing television?
5 Arrange the advantages of television in order – the most important first.
6 Do you think TV is good or bad?

Vocabulary

> Words that sound alike but have different meanings are called **homophones**.

1 **Complete these sentences with the correct word. Discuss each sentence.**

1 John Logie Baird tried _____ (to/too) make diamonds with electricity.
2 John blew up the electricity system of a _____ (hole/whole) town.
3 Television is part of _____ (hour/our) everyday lives.
4 _____ (One/Won) day John invented television.
5 John did not like flying in a _____ (plane/plain).
6 John Logie Baird _____ (made/maid) a glider.

2 **Make up some sentences. Use the words in the box correctly in your sentences.**

too	hole	hour	won	plain	maid

Language building

Remember!

A **compound sentence** can be made up of two **simple sentences**.
A simple sentence can also be called a **main clause**.

(main clause 1)   (conjunction)   (main clause 2)

John Logie Baird experimented   and   he invented television.

Sometimes we can **leave out** the **subject** of the **second** clause.

John Logie Baird experimented and ~~he~~ invented television.

1 **Discuss how to make these pairs of main clauses into compound sentences.
Use *and* or *but* to join them. Write the compound sentences.**

1   John Logie Baird built a glider. He took it onto the roof of his house.
  John Logie Baird built a glider and he took it onto the roof of his house.

2   The inventor failed many times. He did not give up.

3   I like watching television. I don't like listening to the radio.

4   Anna read a book. She made some notes.

5   Kate became a doctor. She worked in a hospital.

6   My teacher started the story. She did not finish it.

7   The children ran all the way. They were late home.

8   Sam did his homework. He went to bed.

2 **Underline the *subject* of the *second main clause* in each of the compound
sentences you wrote. Read each
sentence again and leave it out.**

Does each
compound sentence
still make sense?

Grammar

What is Suzi thinking about?

Suzi's teacher is called Miss Marsh. She is a good teacher and the children in Suzi's class always have to work hard. This term they have been learning about television.

Last week they had to find out about John Logie Baird, the inventor of television. Tomorrow Suzi is going to give a talk. She has had to think very carefully about the advantages and disadvantages of television. Tomorrow afternoon she will have to stand up in front of the whole class. Suzi is very nervous!

1 **What do the children in Suzi's school have to do?**
Ask and answer.

wear a uniform? ✓   Do they have to wear a uniform?   Yes, they do.

be silent in class? ✗   Do they have to be silent in class?   No, they don't.

1 speak politely? ✓   2 learn Russian? ✗   3 work hard? ✓   4 study science? ✓

Now write sentences. Start like this:
They have to …   They do not have to …

2 **When Suzi was preparing her talk, what did she have to do?**
Ask and answer.

go on the Internet? ✓   Did she have to go on the Internet?   Yes, she did.

go to the library? ✗   Did she have to go to the library?   No, she didn't.

1 think carefully? ✓   2 ask her parents? ✗   3 make notes? ✓

Now write sentences. Start like this:
She had to …   She did not have to …

3 **Circle true (T) or false (F).**

1 Suzi will have to give her talk tomorrow.   T   F
2 She will have to stand behind the class.   T   F
3 She will have to speak very quietly.   T   F
4 She will have to forget all her facts.   T   F

Correct the false sentences.

Turn to Fluency Book 5 Programme 15.

   Grammar   *modal verbs – have to, had to, will have to*

Spelling

The **i** in some words sounds like **ee**.
Read the sentences. Listen to the **i** sound in radio.

I like TV. I think it's better than radio.

1 **Say the words. Listen to the sound of the *i* in them.**

radio

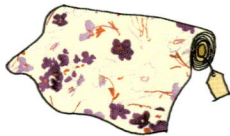

material

champion

audience

mysterious

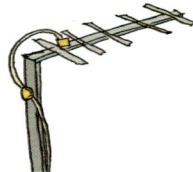

aeriel

obedient

alien

Be a word detective!

2 **Solve these clues using the words above.**

1 someone who wins ___ ___ ___ ___ ___ ___ ___ ___

2 You can listen to this. ___ ___ ___ ___ ___

3 Clothes are made from this. ___ ___ ___ ___ ___ ___ ___ ___

4 This comes from outer space! ___ ___ ___ ___ ___

5 This is very strange. ___ ___ ___ ___ ___ ___ ___ ___ ___ ___

6 This helps you get a good picture on your TV. ___ ___ ___ ___ ___ ___

7 These people watch a show. ___ ___ ___ ___ ___ ___ ___ ___

8 This means to do as you are told. ___ ___ ___ ___ ___ ___ ___ ___

Class writing

When you express your **point of view** it is important that you make your **opinions** clear. It is also important to think about other people's points of view and to be as **fair** as possible.

1. **Discuss what sort of fast food can you buy in your country.**

2. **As a class, make a list of the advantages and disadvantages of fast food.**

Advantages	Disadvantages
It is very cheap.	It is high in calories.

3. **Have a class vote.**
   Decide if you think fast food is good for you or not.

4. **Write an argument in favour of (or against) fast food.**
   Support the point of view of most people in the class.

Read the talk the girl gave on TV on page 127 again. Follow these tips to help you with your writing.

- State your point of view clearly at the beginning.
- Begin a new paragraph. Give several reasons to support your point of view.
- Begin another paragraph. Be fair. Give one or two reasons which support the opposite point of view.
- Write a final paragraph. State one or two more reasons which support the majority of your class' opinion.

Reading for enrichment

Albert the TV Addict

There are dangers in watching too much television! Read this story about Albert and see!

Albert was a lovely old man. He loved children and always had time to talk to his neighbours. The only time he felt lonely was in the evening. Then Albert had an idea. 'I'll get a television,' he said.

Albert thought it was wonderful. The soap operas! The sports! The films! The advertisements!

Then Albert became frustrated. While he was watching one channel, he was missing what was on the other channels. He bought a DVD recorder to solve the problem.

Then he realised there was another problem. When he wanted to eat he had to leave his TV and go into the kitchen to prepare his meals. So he got a microwave. He moved this and his fridge into the bedroom. Now he didn't have to move anymore – unless he wanted to go to the bathroom!

Albert spent all his money on televisions. He even sold his lovely garden – he didn't have time to do any gardening anyway! With the money he bought a new satellite dish. He also bought four new televisions and an extra DVD recorder!

Soon his whole house was full of televisions. He could watch ten TV programmes at the same time! Albert didn't go out anymore. 'It's a boring old world!' Albert muttered as he switched channels with his remote control. Within a few weeks Albert had changed from being a friendly old man to being a miserable old man. He never saw anyone. He never talked to anyone. He stayed indoors and watched TV every minute of the day. Albert had become a TV addict!

Moral:	Watching TV for a short time each day is fine but too much TV can be bad for you!

A night in the jungle

We moved into the jungle. Old Mali, my guide, preceded me. He went in front and carried an axe and I followed close behind him. The path was covered over with branches and bushes. I had no idea where I was.

We stopped for the night. We put our bags on the ground in a small clearing. There was a stream at the edge of the clearing. We could get our drinking water from the stream. The guide lit a fire. When it was burning, he showed me how to make a bed with soft moss. Then he helped me make my bed on the other side of the fire. It was soft and comfortable.

'This bed is more comfortable than my bed at home,' I said. Old Mali just laughed quietly in reply.

'We need enough wood to keep the fire going all night,' he said. I jumped up quickly. 'I will help you,' I replied.

We went off into the jungle to collect as much wood as possible. The guide said that we must have some large pieces of wood. 'They last longer and the fire must burn all night. We must have a fire to keep away any animals that come near. All animals are afraid of fire, aren't they?'

It was almost dark by the time we finished. We put the huge pile of wood beside Old Mali's bed so that he could reach it easily during the night. He would be able to pick up the wood and put it on the fire without getting out of bed.

When we finished our supper, the guide got onto his bed and lay down. It was now completely dark. In the firelight Old Mali seemed to be fast asleep on his bed. I suddenly felt alone and afraid. I wished he would wake up and share my loneliness.

Stimulus narrative story

The jungle was a wall of blackness in the light of the fire. From far away in this blackness I heard the crying of a jackal. I felt frightened and suddenly my mouth went dry. I really wished the guide would wake up. I wanted to scream. I felt my mouth opening wide, ready to scream as loud as possible. I breathed deeply and was just about to scream out in fear. But I did not scream. I saw Old Mali's face in the firelight. This made me feel ashamed. If I screamed, he would know I was afraid.

I held my teeth tightly together to stop myself from screaming. I lay down on my comfortable bed and closed my eyes. As soon as I closed my eyes, I heard a thousand noises. The whole jungle became alive with animals creeping all around me. I opened my eyes and jumped out of bed. I pulled my knife out and held it above my head. I was sure I was going to see a wild jackal beside the fire. All I saw was the guide who was now lying on his side with his eyes wide open.

'You can put your knife away now,' he said quietly. 'It is time to go to sleep, isn't it? You have a long day ahead of you tomorrow.'

Old Mali's calm voice made me feel better. I got back into bed and lay down. I closed my eyes and, knowing he was watching, I soon fell fast asleep.

Comprehension

1 **Number the sentences in the correct order.**

_____ We stopped for the night.
__1__ We went into the jungle.
_____ I heard a thousand noises.
_____ The guide lit a fire.
_____ I pulled my knife out.
_____ I got back into bed and soon fell fast asleep.
_____ We had our supper.
_____ I lay down on my bed and closed my eyes.
_____ We collected firewood.
_____ I opened my eyes and jumped out of bed.
_____ The guide spoke to me quietly and calmly.

2 **Discuss your answers to these questions.**

1 Did the guide know where he was going and what he was doing?
2 What do you think they had in their bags?
3 Why was it important to   a be near a stream?   b light a fire?
4 How do you know they stopped for the night in the evening?
5 What does this mean: 'The jungle was a wall of blackness.'?
6 Do you think this was really true: 'The whole jungle became alive with animals creeping all around me.'?
7 How does the author make this story exciting?

Vocabulary

> Remember! A **synonym** is a word that means the **same** as another word.

1 **Find these words in the story. Write a _synonym_ for each word. Use the thesaurus on page 166 to help you.**

1 preceded	_____	2 guide	_____
3 ashamed	_____	4 finished	_____
5 comfortable	_____	6 afraid	_____
7 wide	_____	8 calm	_____

2 **Now think of an _antonym_ for each word above. Remember! An _antonym_ is a word with the _opposite_ meaning. Write in your copy book. Use the thesaurus on page 166 to help you.**

Language building

> Remember! We can write **speech** in **two** ways:
> as **direct speech** or as **reported speech**.

Old Mali said, 'The fire is near my bed.'

This is written in **direct** speech. Old Mali's **exact** words are used. Speech marks are used.

Old Mali said that the fire was near his bed.

This is written in **reported** speech. Old Mali's exact words are **not** used. **No** speech marks are used.

1 Read these sentences. The first sentence in each pair is in direct speech. The second sentence is in reported speech. Discuss what differences you can see in each pair of sentences.

1 Old Mali said, 'I need some wood for the fire.'
   Old Mali said that he needed some wood for the fire.
2 Jeff said, 'My bed of moss is very comfortable.'
   Jeff said that his bed of moss was very comfortable.
3 Jeff said, 'I am frightened of the dark.'
   Jeff said that he was frightened of the dark.
4 'What are you worried about?' Old Mali asked Jeff.
   Old Mali asked Jeff what he was worried about.
5 'I don't like wild animals,' Jeff replied.
   Jeff replied that he didn't like wild animals.

2 Discuss which sentences contain direct speech (D) or reported speech (R).

1 'It's time to go to sleep,' Old Mali said. _____
2 Jeff told Old Mali that he wasn't tired. _____
3 'I want to go home,' Jeff cried. _____
4 'There are no wild animals in this jungle,' Old Mali said to Jeff. _____
5 Jeff said that he heard the sound of a snake. _____
6 Old Mali told Jeff that it was the sound of the trees. _____

Grammar

What do you remember about the night in the jungle?

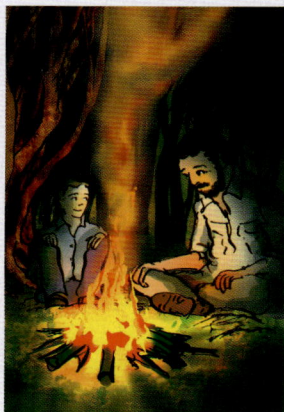

Old Mali and the boy stopped for the night. Mali lit a fire. The boy sat and listened to the sounds of the jungle.

- It's noisy in the jungle, isn't it?
  - Many creatures come out at night.
- They're not dangerous, are they?
  - Well, there are snakes and jackals. And tigers.
- Tigers?
  - What's the matter? You're not scared, are you?
- But we're a long way from the town, aren't we?
  - Don't worry. I am your guide. You are safe with me.

1 **Ask and answer. Agree with the speaker.**

It's noisy in the jungle, isn't it? | Yes, it is.

It isn't cold in the jungle, is it? | No, it isn't.

1 It's hot in the jungle, isn't it?
2 Mali is a good guide, isn't he?
3 Jackals are not dangerous, are they?
4 Tigers are dangerous, aren't they?
5 You're not afraid of the dark, are you?
6 We're feeling OK, aren't we?

2 **Complete these sentences. Use the words in the box.**

1 It's a lovely day today, _____
2 We're working hard, _____
3 That boy is English, _____
4 His mother isn't from London, _____
5 You're not tired, _____
6 Elephants aren't dangerous, _____

is she?
aren't we?
are you?
isn't it?
are they?
isn't he?

Don't forget the question marks!

3 **Complete these sentences.**

1 Some snakes are poisonous, _____
2 The boy is not in danger, _____
3 The jungle is not quiet at night, _____

Turn to Fluency Book 5 Programme 16.

Spelling

A **prefix** is a group of letters we put at the **beginning** of a word.
Pre and **mis** are two common prefixes.

The guide **pre**ceded me.
(The guide went in front of me.)

The prefix **pre** often means
in front of or **before**.

The boy **mis**behaved.
(The boy behaved badly.)

The prefix **mis** often means
badly or **wrong**.

1 **Make these words. Read the words you make.**

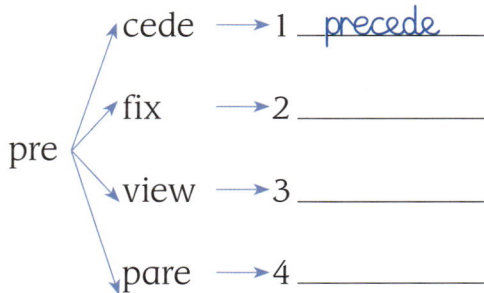

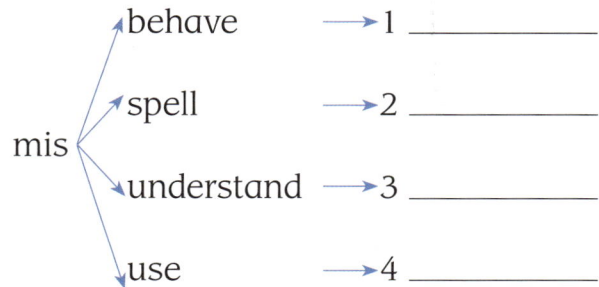

pre
- cede → 1 _precede_
- fix → 2 _____
- view → 3 _____
- pare → 4 _____

mis
- behave → 1 _____
- spell → 2 _____
- understand → 3 _____
- use → 4 _____

2 **Discuss which *pre* word means:**

1   a group of letters you can put at the beginning of a word.
2   to look at something before anyone else can see it.
3   to get things ready.
4   to go in front of someone.

3 **Discuss which *mis* word means:**

1   to spell a word wrong.
2   to use something in the wrong way.
3   not to understand something.
4   to behave badly.

Class writing

The **characters** in a story are very important.
We can learn a lot about a character:
- by what the author tells us about him or her
- by the way the author describes him or her (and from pictures of the character)
- by the things the character says or the way in which he or she says them
- by the way the character behaves and the things he or she does.

1 **Make some notes on the board about Old Mali, the guide. Use the headings below to help you.**

If the information is not in the story or you can't see it in a picture, guess it!

- Name:
- Physical appearance (how he looks):
  age
  height
  face
  clothes
  anything else?
- Job (what he does)
- Skills (what he's good at doing)
- Personality (the sort of person he is, e.g. quiet, helpful)
- Relationships (how he gets on with the boy; the way he talks to him, etc.)

2 **Now describe Old Mali.**

I have started it for you!

Old Mali is a guide. He guides people through the forest. He always carries an axe to clear a path and to cut down bushes. He is about 45 years old.

When you have finished, read your description together and edit it.
Can you improve it?
Do you want to:
- leave anything out?
- move any sentences to a different position?
- add any more describing words?

Reading for enrichment

Your five senses

You can see, hear, touch, smell and taste. Seeing, hearing, touching, smelling and tasting are called your five senses. You need your senses to help you live.

What colours can you see around you? What sounds can you hear? Run your hand over your desk. Is it smooth or rough? You can answer these questions because of messages your brain gets from your different senses. How does your brain get these messages? Read the passage and find out!

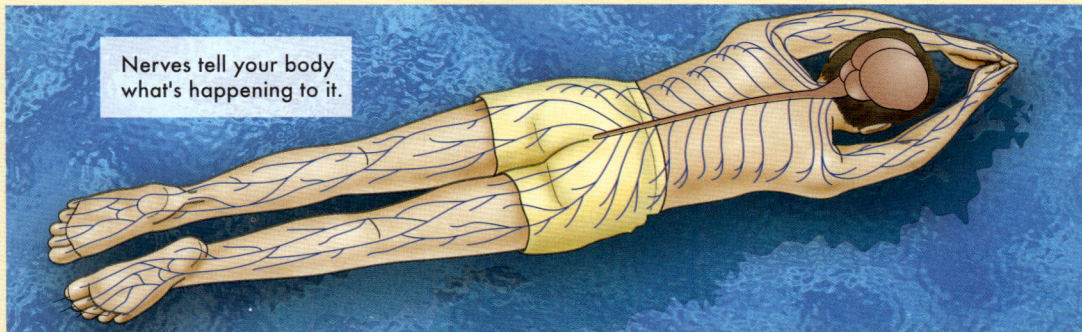

People who do not have one or more of their senses find life a lot more difficult. Try to imagine what your life would be like if you were blind or deaf. Life would not be very easy.

You need your senses to protect you and to help you enjoy life. With your eyes you can read these words and see a beautiful sunset. Your nose tells you if a smell is pleasant or unpleasant. Your sense of taste helps you to enjoy good food. When a car sounds its horn your ears tell you of danger. Your ears also bring you the joy of music.

Through the whole of your body there is a system of nerves. These nerves carry messages to and from your brain. Each of your senses collects information called sensations from around you. This information is sent to your brain through your nerves. When your brain gets a message from one of your senses, it sends back a message to a part of your body and tells it how to react. For example, if you prick your finger with a pin, your nerves send a message to your brain and your brain tells you to pull your finger away from the pin.

Your brain is like a huge computer. It is the control centre of your body. It decides what you need to do and gives you orders to do it.

Nerves tell your body what's happening to it.

How your ear works

When I was small, I used to lie in bed and listen to the sound of the television in the living room.

When I was small, I used to lie in bed and listen to the sound of the wind blowing in the trees.

We *hear* sounds. They travel through the air. Put your hand in front of your mouth and speak or sing. You can *feel* the air moving. When something makes a sound, the noise makes the air vibrate. These vibrations are called sound waves. If you pluck a string on a guitar you can see it vibrate as it makes a sound.

Look at the shape of your friend's ear. Its shape helps it to catch sound waves and send them down the ear canal.

Did you know that you have a drum in your ear? Your ear drum is a bit of thin skin which moves very quickly when sound waves hit it.

Your ear drum is joined to three tiny bones. When your ear drum moves, it makes these three tiny bones move, too. These bones are the smallest in your body. One of them is about two millimetres from one end to the other. It is small enough to sit on top of a pin!

Inside your ear you also have three tubes. They contain watery liquid. When the three tiny bones move, they make the watery liquid move, too.

A nerve then carries this 'sound wave message' to your brain. Your brain tells you what the sound is.

The watery liquid inside these tubes in your ear also helps you to balance. When you spin round quickly this makes the liquid in these tubes move about too quickly. When you stop spinning you feel dizzy. You have to stand still for a few moments. The world still seems to be spinning around! This is because the liquid in the tubes continues to spin round for a short time.

This **picture diagram** helps explain how your ear works.

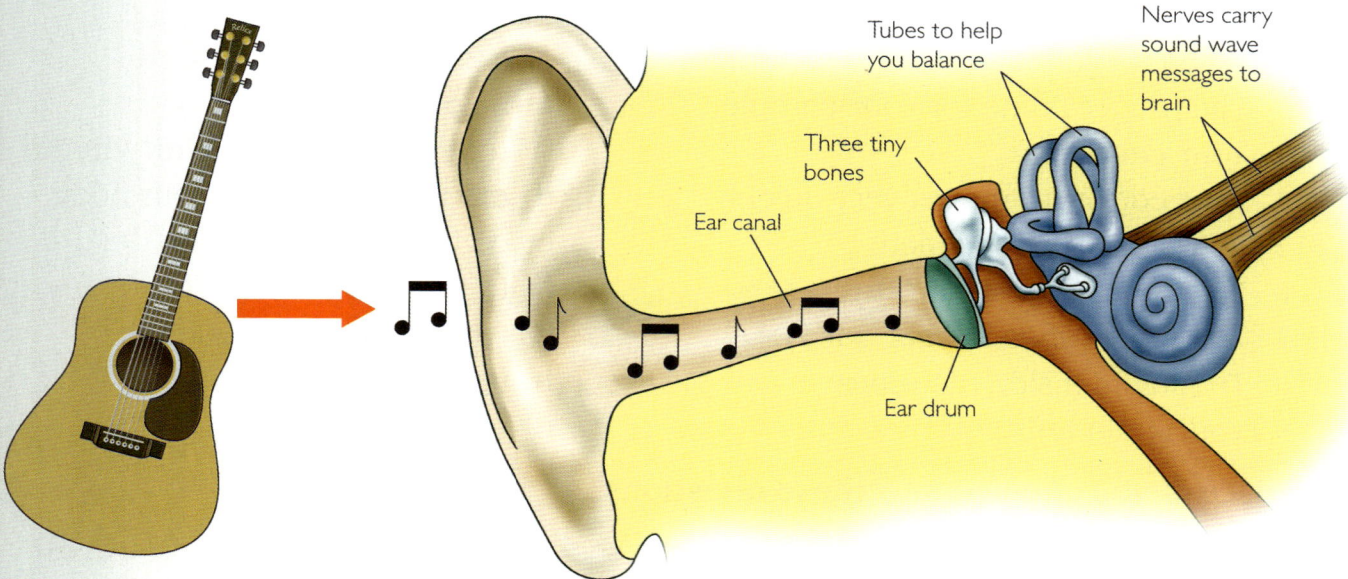

Tubes to help you balance

Nerves carry sound wave messages to brain

Three tiny bones

Ear canal

Ear drum

This **flow diagram** also helps explain how your ear works.

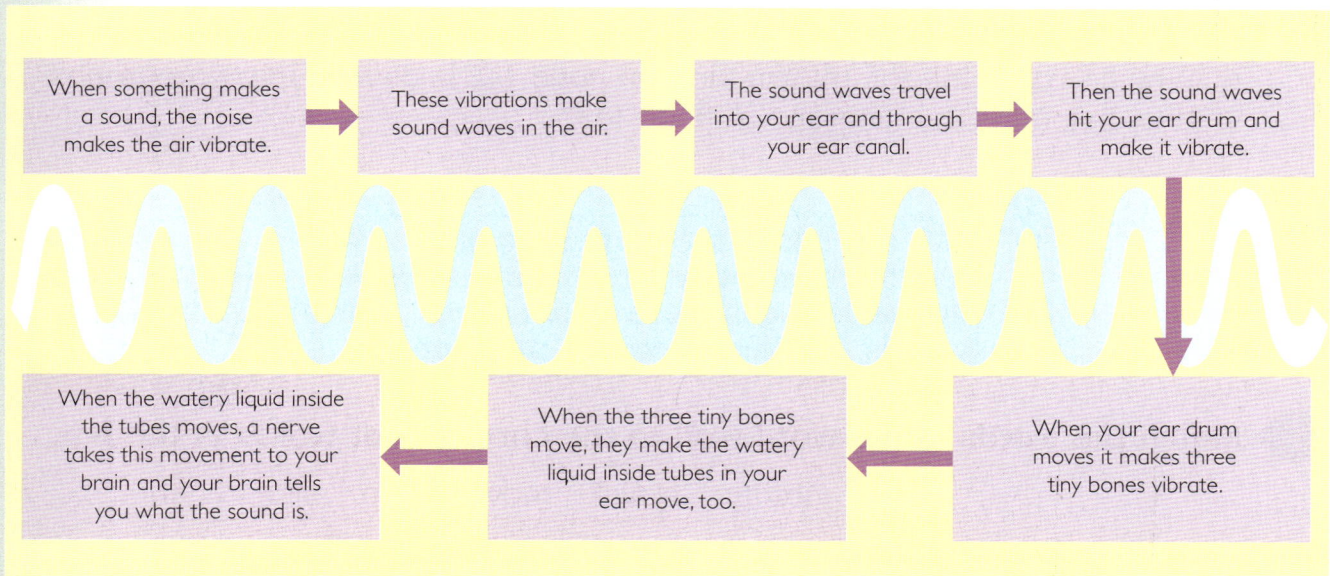

When something makes a sound, the noise makes the air vibrate.	These vibrations make sound waves in the air.	The sound waves travel into your ear and through your ear canal.	Then the sound waves hit your ear drum and make it vibrate.

When the watery liquid inside the tubes moves, a nerve takes this movement to your brain and your brain tells you what the sound is.	When the three tiny bones move, they make the watery liquid inside tubes in your ear move, too.	When your ear drum moves it makes three tiny bones vibrate.

Comprehension

1 Match the beginning and ending of each sentence.

1	When something makes a sound,	____	a	is a bit of thin skin.
2	The proper name for your earhole	____	b	help you to balance.
3	Your ear drum	____	c	the noise makes the air vibrate.
4	Your ear drum moves very quickly	____	d	are the smallest in your body.
5	Your ear drum is joined	____	e	contain watery liquid.
6	The bones in your ear drum	____	f	to three tiny bones.
7	The three tubes in your ear	____	g	when sound waves hit it.
8	The liquid inside the tubes	____	h	is your ear canal.
9	Your brain tells you	____	i	what a sound is.

2 Discuss your answers to these questions.

1 Look at your friend's ear. Why does the shape of it help it catch sound waves?
2 Why do you think the thin skin in your ear is called a drum?
3 What is interesting about the bones in your ear?
4 Explain why you feel dizzy when you spin around.
5 How helpful are the pictures on page 143?
6 Why do you think the information on page 142 is divided into paragraphs?
7 How helpful is the diagram on page 143?

Vocabulary

> We can add to the **beginning** or **ending** of some words to make them **longer**. We call these words **root** words, e.g. hear: **hear**ing, mis**hear**.

1 Match the words in the word wall to the correct root words in the box.

hear   vibrate   travel   move   help   side

vibration	helpless	outside	movement
unhelpful	hearing	traveller	mishear
vibrates	travelled	remove	inside

2 Make up some sentences. Use the words in the word wall. Write in your copy book.

Language building

We can change some **verbs** into **nouns** by adding a **suffix**.

(verb)   (noun)

The strings of a guitar **vibrate**. The **vibration** of the air is called a sound wave.

1 Match the noun to the verb.

verbs	nouns
1 vibrate _c_	a advertisement
2 evaporate ____	b education
3 advertise ____	c vibration
4 agree ____	d enjoyment
5 educate ____	e improvement
6 enjoy ____	f evaporation
7 improve ____	g decoration
8 decorate ____	h agreement

2 Write the correct *tion* noun to complete these sentences.

1 We go to school to get an _____ .

2 A noise is made by the _____ of the air.

3 When water changes into water vapour, it is called _____ .

4 The _____ on the girl's dress was very pretty.

3 Write the correct *verb* or *noun* to complete these sentences.

1 The _____ (advertise/advertisement) on the TV was very funny.

2 I tried hard to _____ (improve/improvement) my spelling.

3 I _____ (agree/agreement) that sport is good for you.

4 Reading books gives me a lot of _____ (enjoy/enjoyment).

Grammar

What did Alfie hear every night?

When Alfie was small, his family lived in a house by the sea. At night he *used to* lie in bed and listen to the sound of the waves on the sand. He *used to* listen to the wind blowing in the trees. He *used to* listen to the owls hooting in the dark.

But now Alfie's family lives in the city and at night he hears different sounds. He *used to* hear owls hooting. Now he hears cars hooting. He *used to* hear the roar of the sea. Now he hears the roar of the traffic.

1 Correct these sentences.

1 When Alfie was small, he used to live in the mountains.
2 At night he used to stand at his window and listen to the sea.
3 He used to listen to the waves on the rocks.
4 He used to hear the wind rattling the windows.
5 He used to hear cars hooting.

2 Complete these sentences with *used to* and a verb from the box.

> travel   work   live   visit   be

Here are Alfie's grandparents.
They have an apartment in the city but they _____ _____ in a house in the country. Grandma _____ _____ a teacher and Grandpa _____ _____ as a doctor. These days they have a nice car but years ago they _____ _____ in a horse and cart. Alfie _____ _____ them in the holidays but now he can see them every day.

3 Write about when you were small.

1 When I was small I used to _____
2 I _____
3 I _____

Turn to Fluency Book 5 Programme 17.

Spelling

world

When or comes after w it often sounds like er.

warm

When ar comes after w it often sounds like or.

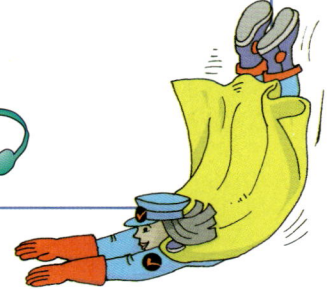

1 Talk about the pictures. Read the words.
Write the correct word for each picture.

warm or worm?	wardrobe or world?	word or work?	reward or swarm?
1 _____	2 _____	3 _____	4 _____
swarm or warn?	warm or warn?	world or word?	world or worse?
5 _____	6 _____	7 _____	8 _____
	warm or worse?	worse or work?	
	9 _____	10 _____	

2 Write the words.
ar words _____ _____ _____ _____ _____
or words _____ _____ _____ _____ _____

3 Read each set of words above. Listen to the *ar* and *or* sounds in them.

4 Make up some sentences. Use each word in them. Write in your copy book.

Class writing

When we write information it is important to **explain** things clearly.

1 Look at the diagrams and notes below. They explain about how we breathe.

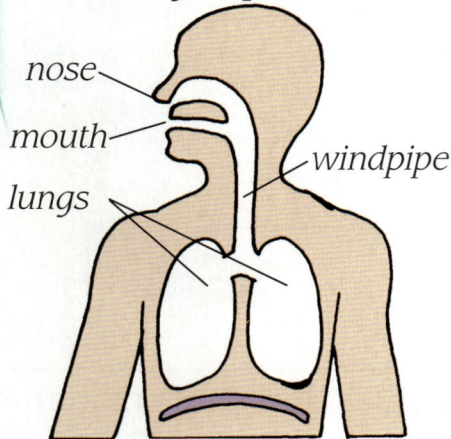

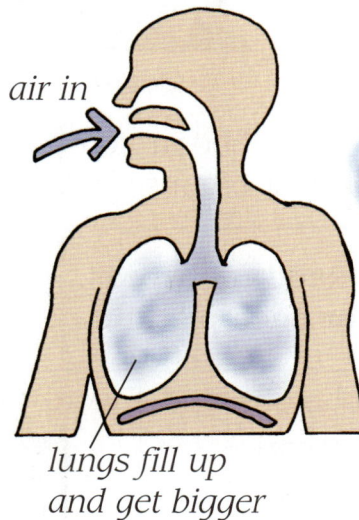

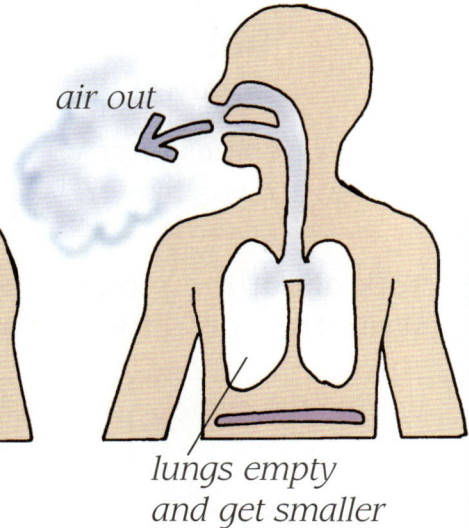

nose
mouth
lungs
windpipe

air in

lungs fill up and get bigger

air out

lungs empty and get smaller

air – contains oxygen
need to breathe – to live
need oxygen – to grow
air – in – nose and mouth
air – down windpipe to lungs
lungs – suck air in – push air out
breathe in – lungs fill – get bigger
breathe out – lungs empty – get smaller

2 Now write and explain how we breathe. Do it together on the board.

Use the notes and diagrams to help you. These questions will help you, too.

When you have finished, think of a good **title** for your explanation.

- What does the air we breathe contain?
- Why do we need to breathe?
- How does air get into our bodies?
- Where does the air go?
- How do our lungs work?

Writing **explanatory texts and diagrams**

Reading for enrichment

My Hands

Think of all my hands can do,
pick up a pin and do up a shoe,
they can help, they can hurt, too,
or paint a summer sky bright blue.

They can throw and they can catch.
They clap the team that wins the match.
If I'm rough my hands can scratch.
If I'm rude my hands can snatch.

Gently, gently they can stroke,
carefully carry a glass of Coke,
tickle my best friend for a joke,
but I won't let them nip and poke.

My hands give and my hands take.
With Gran they bake a yummy cake.
They can mend and they can break.
Think of music hands can make.

Jo Peters

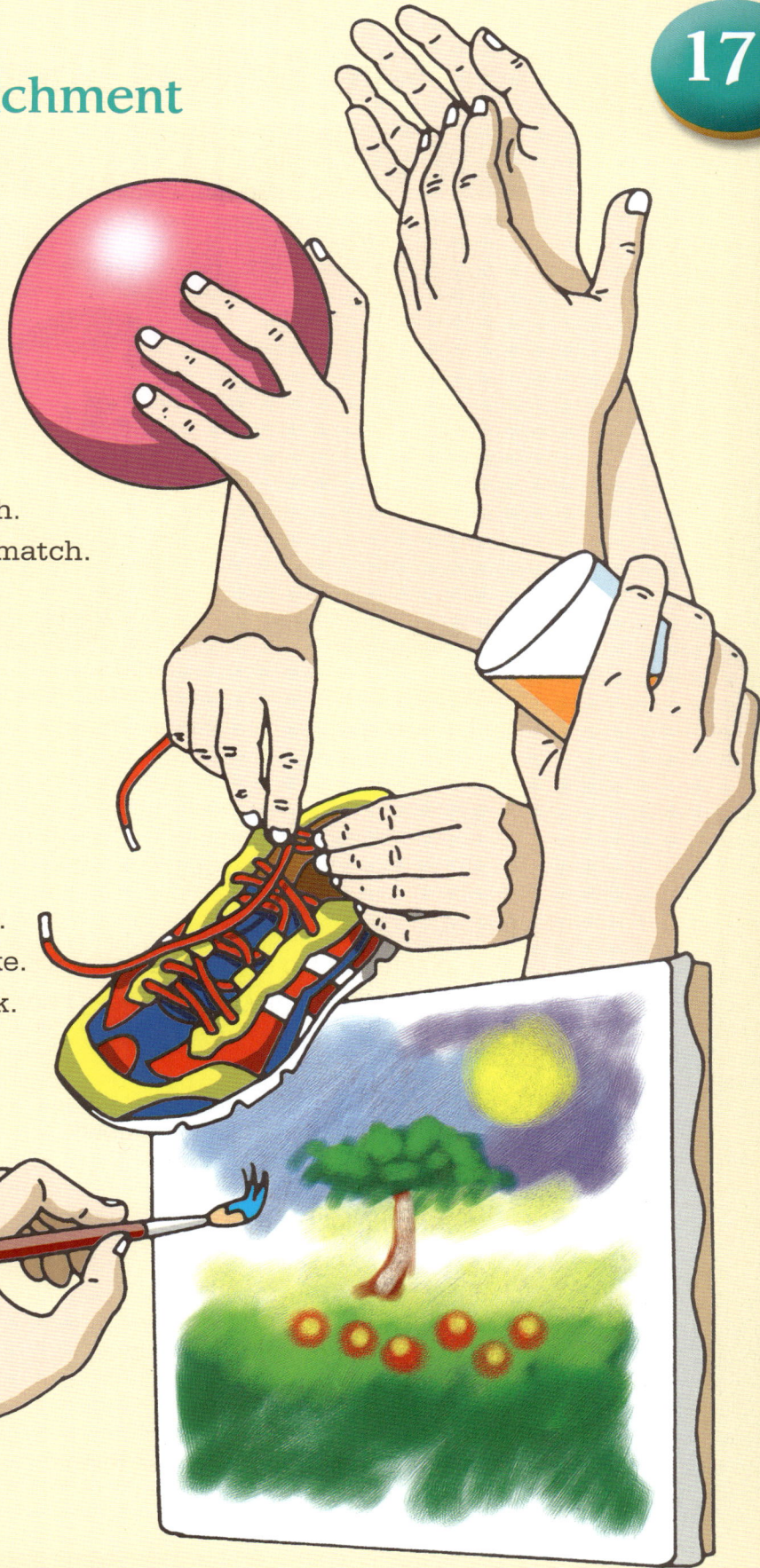

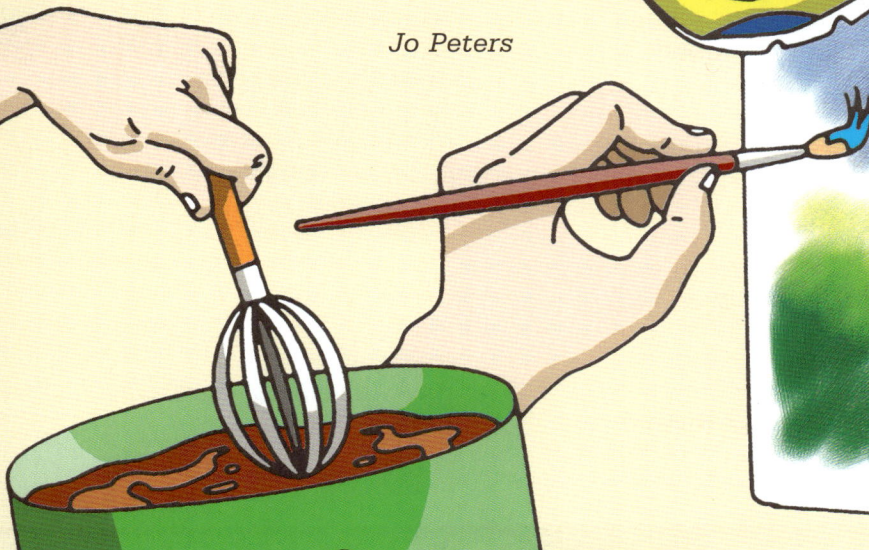

The Five Senses Shop

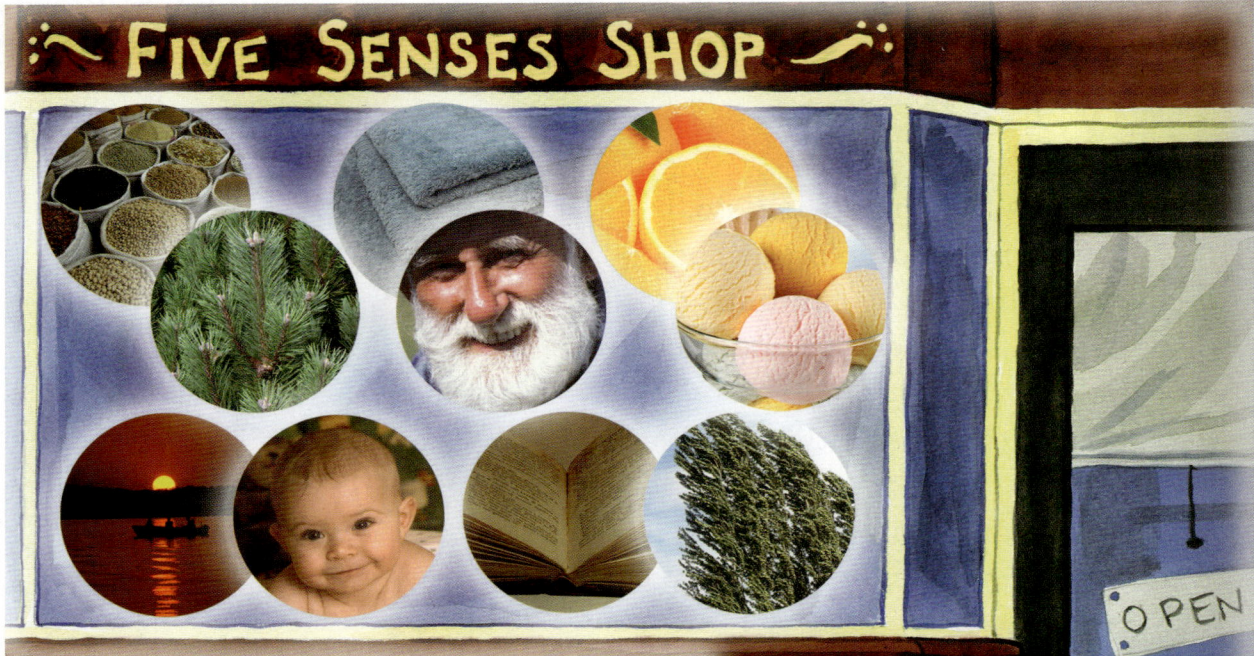

Do you know a shop that sells these things?

The smell of:
- pine trees in a forest,
- spices on a market stall.

The feel of:
- a soft towel to dry yourself after a bath,
- the bristles of my grandfather's beard.

The taste of:
- a sweet, juicy orange,
- ice cream melting in your mouth.

The sight of:
- a beautiful sunset,
- a baby's first smile.

The sound of:
- a page of a book turning over,
- the sigh of the wind.

Do you know a shop that sells these things?
Then tell me where it is, please do!

The Sounds of the Night

Jump in bed,
Turn out the light,
Shut your eyes
Really tight.
Listen to the
Sounds of the night.

A chinking noise - what can that be?
Someone making a cup of tea?
My sister splashing about in the bath,
Mum and Dad downstairs enjoying a laugh.
The wind rustling in the trees,
The loudness of my brother's sneeze!
A chair scraping on the floor,
A visitor knocking at the door.
Distant voices, softly speaking,
The wooden stairs groaning and creaking.
Raindrops running down the window-pane,
A dog barking again and again.
A car hooting, a plane in the sky –
I just can't sleep – I wonder why!

Jump in bed,
Turn out the light,
Shut your eyes
Really tight.
Listen to the
Sounds of the night.

Comprehension

1 **Answer these questions about 'The Five Senses Shop'.**

1 Which sense is missing?   smell   taste   sight   hearing
2 What   a smells   b tastes   c sounds   does the shop sell?

2 **Now answer these questions about 'The Sounds of the Night'.**

1 a How many lines has the chorus got? b How many lines has the verse got?
2 Where is the poet?
3 What is the poet doing?
4 Which words rhyme with a light? b be?   c bath?   d trees?   e floor?
   f speaking?   g window-paine?   h sky?

3 **Discuss 'The Five Senses Shop' poem.**

1 Would you like to visit this shop? Why (or why not)?
2 Go through each sense one at a time and discuss some other things you
   would like to find in the shop.
3 The poem does not rhyme. Is this important?

4 **Now discuss 'The Sounds of the Night' poem.**

1 Do you think the title describes the poem well?
2 Do you think you can hear things better if you shut your eyes?
3 What would life be like without sound?
4 What did you like (or dislike) about the poem?

Vocabulary

> Some words tell us about the **sounds things make**. In 'The Sounds of the Night' there are lots of these words.

1 **What sound does each of the following things in the poem make:**
   a making a cup of tea   b my sister   c the wind   d my brother
   e a chair   f the wooden stairs   g a dog   h a car

2 **Think of some other things that make these sounds:**
   a chinking   b rustling   c scraping   d groaning   e creaking
   f splashing   g hooting

Language building

A **sentence tag** is something extra we add to the **beginning** or the **end** of a sentence.

Always use a comma **before** or **after** a sentence tag.

> I like the sound of a clock ticking, don't you?

> Yes, I do.

1 **Where does the comma go? Write these sentences correctly.**

1 Come here Tom.   _____
2 Can I have a drink please?   _____
3 I can't eat that cake can I?   _____
4 I want an apple a green apple.   _____

> They all end with a sentence tag.

2 **Where does the comma go? Write these sentences correctly.**

1 Anna where are you? _____
2 Oh no I hate the taste of cabbage! _____
3 Sorry I didn't know you were behind me. _____
4 Oh good I thought we were going to be late! _____

> They all begin with a sentence tag.

3 **Put in the missing commas in this little play. Underline the sentence tag in each sentence.**

Teacher: Have you done your homework Amy?

Amy: Yes I have.

Teacher: Well where is it?

Amy: It's in my bag I think.

Teacher: This is your bag isn't it?

Amy: My bag isn't blue it's red.

Teacher: I can't see a red bag can you?

Amy: Oh dear I think I left my bag at home!

Grammar

Look at Sally and Ben! What have they been doing?

Sally and her little brother, Ben, looked at themselves in the mirror. They were covered in mud. Sally washed Ben's face and hands before handing him a towel. 'Dry yourself with this,' she said. Then she washed and dried herself.

When Dad came home and saw the beautiful garden, he was very surprised. 'Did you do this, Sally?' he asked. 'I didn't do it by myself,' answered Sally. 'Ben helped me.' 'Well,' said Dad, 'it looks wonderful. You should be very proud of yourselves.'

1 **Answer these questions.**

1 Did Sally and Ben look at themselves in the bathroom mirror?
2 Did Sally wash herself first or second?
3 What did she use to dry herself?
4 How did Dad feel when he saw the garden?
5 What do you think the garden was like before?
6 What did Dad say to the children?

2 **Read and match the sentences.**

1 Your face is covered in mud, Ben. ____
2 We've worked really hard. ____
3 Do you like this cake? ____
4 John did not pass his exams. ____
5 The horse can't walk. ____

a I think it has hurt itself.
b I made it myself.
c He felt very angry with himself.
d We can be proud of ourselves!
e Look at yourself in the mirror!

3 **Choose the correct words to complete these sentences.**

1 'Where am I?' the man asked_____ .   (himself/herself)
2 Go away! I can do this by_____ .   (yourself/myself)
3 If you eat all that cake, you'll make_____ ill. (itself/yourself)
4 The children are old enough to dress _____ .   (themselves/ourselves)
5 You can all be very pleased with_____ .   (yourself/yourselves)

Turn to Fluency Book 5 Programme 18.

Spelling

Homophones are words that **sound the same** but have got **different meanings**.

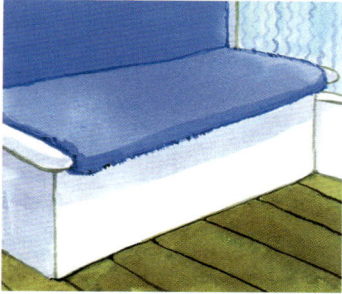

a stair

a stare

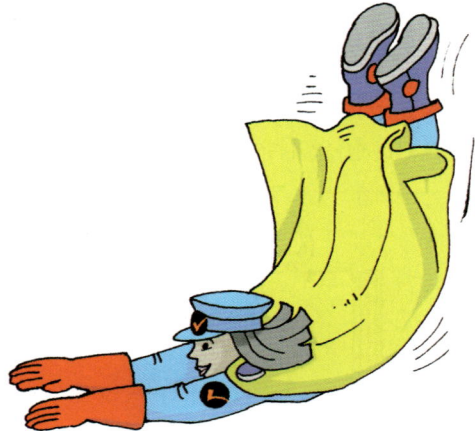

1 **Match the pairs of *homophones*. Write them.**

1 pair	c	a peace	1 *pair, pear*
2 road	___	b knows	2 _____
3 piece	___	c pear	3 _____
4 nose	___	d weight	4 _____
5 wait	___	e plane	5 _____
6 write	___	f steel	6 _____
7 steal	___	g rode	7 _____
8 plain	___	h right	8 _____

2 **Underline the correct word.**

1	a fruit	<u>pear</u>	pair
2	a place for cars	rode	road
3	quiet	piece	peace
4	a part of your face	nose	knows
5	how heavy something is	wait	weight
6	correct	write	right
7	a sort of metal	steal	steel
8	something that flies in the sky	plane	plain

Class writing

I love list poems!

In a **list poem** you think of a subject and write your ideas in an interesting way. You do not need to worry about making the poem rhyme!
Do you like the start of my list poem?

I love to see:

the first rays of the morning sun,
my footprints in the sand,
my soft bed waiting for me when
I'm tired,

1 Brainstorm and write on the board some things you all love to see.

2 Vote and choose five to ten of the best ideas.

3 Read each idea again.

- Can you write it in a better way – or are you happy with it?
- Can you add any describing words to make it more interesting?

4 Now write your class list poem.

Look back at 'The Five Senses Shop' list poem on page 150.
Notice how it ends with an interesting question and sentence.
Think of a good way to end your class poem.

Reading for enrichment

The Old Man and the Strong Man

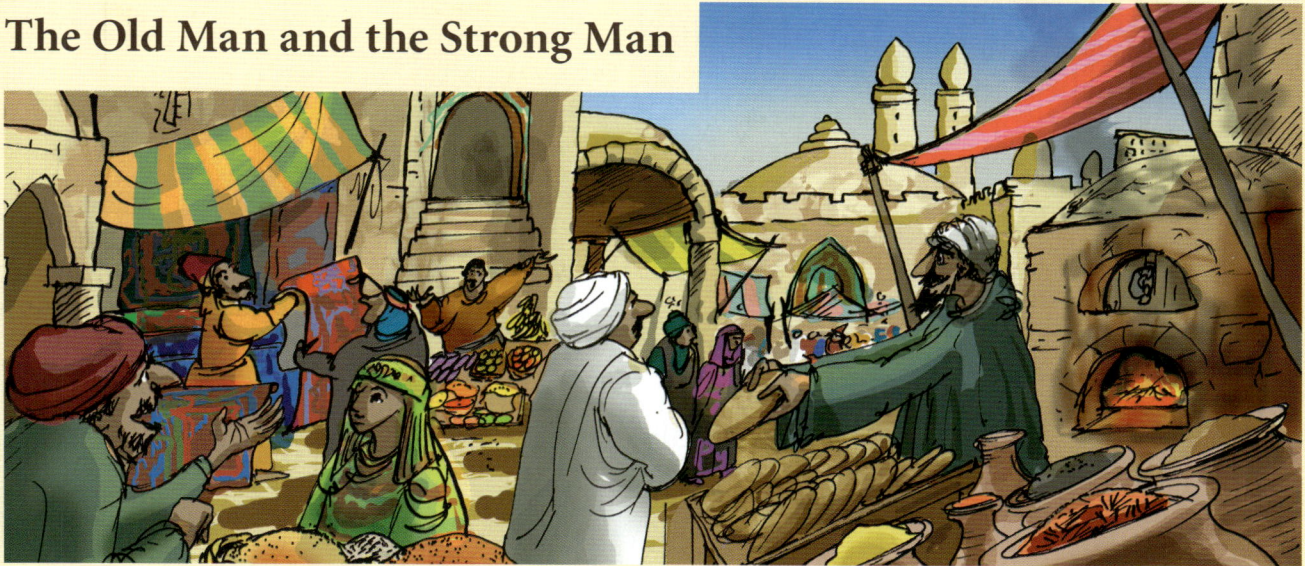

Long ago there was a town with a busy market place. The market was full of noise. People were standing in groups and talking to each other; stallholders were shouting and trying to persuade people to buy things from their stalls. The market was full of colour – purple aubergines, red and green apples, yellow bananas, brilliant coloured spices and brightly-patterned carpets. The market was full of smells – food cooking on fires, fresh fruit and bread being baked. People came to buy and sell all sorts of things in the market.

One day an old man went to the market to buy some vegetables. He saw a crowd of people. In the middle of them was a strong man. Everyone was afraid of him. The strong man had a big heavy weight.

The strong man said, 'Look at me. I can easily lift this heavy weight.' He bent down and took hold of the heavy weight. He pulled and pulled. His face went redder and redder. Slowly he lifted the weight above his head. 'I am the strongest man in the world,' he cried. 'I challenge anyone to pick it up.' He laughed nastily at the crowd. Some people tried to lift it but it was too heavy for them. Most of the people turned away.

Then a brave person at the back of the crowd shouted, 'You are just like an ox! An ox is strong too, but it has no sense!' The people all laughed. The old man smiled.

The strong man was angry. He saw the old man smiling. 'Why are you smiling?' he shouted at him. The old man said, 'You may be strong but you are very proud. You do not know how to laugh at yourself.' The strong man felt foolish. He looked down at the ground and walked away. After that, no-one was afraid of him anymore.

Revision 4

1 **Look at the picture.**
Have you seen things like these anywhere in books or films?
How old do you think these things are?

2 **Listen and read.** 🎧

3 **Read and answer.**
1 Where was the car engine?
2 How fast did it go?
3 Is the computer a real one?
4 When did people start to take colour photographs?
5 What were the first TV pictures like?
6 Who rode the bike with the big wheel?
7 How many pieces has the telephone got?
8 What do you do with a gramophone?
9 What did you do first to make the sound come out?

Where's the engine?

Look underneath, Peter.

a

Oh. It's not very big, is it? Did it go fast?

Quite fast. It went at about 30 kilometres an hour.

Screens used to be very small.

The pictures weren't in black and white, were they?

Yes, they were!

c

You had to hold this piece to your ear and speak into this. Don't drop it, Susie.

d

It's a gramophone.

What do you do with it?

You listen to it. The sound came out here.

f

First turn the handle, Joe. I'll show you.

This is a model of one of the first computers. It was made in America.

It's huge, isn't it, Grandpa?

Yes. Don't touch it, Freddy.

b

Be careful, Billy. It's very big and heavy.

e

Did they used to take colour photos with this?

No, colour photography is only 70 years old.

Look at the funny bike, Grandma. It is a bicycle, isn't it?

Yes, it is.

Who used to ride this?

A man rode it. Ladies didn't ride bikes like this.

g

4 Listen and say which object they are looking at. 🎧

1 _____
2 _____
3 _____
4 _____
5 _____
6 _____
7 _____

5 What did they tell them to do, or not do?

_____
_____
_____
_____
_____
_____

6 Act out the scene.

159

Dictionary

abseiling   sport of going down a steep rock face using ropes

action   something that you do

active   always doing things

activities   enjoyable, interesting things which people do

advantage   a good feature something has

adventure   an exciting time

advert   short for advertisement – something in a newspaper or on the television to persuade people to buy something or go somewhere

advice   an opinion that is given to you, telling you what is best

alien   a being from outer space

amazing   wonderful

ancient   very old

anxious   worried

archery   sport of shooting arrows from a bow

ashamed   to feel guilty or embarrassed about something

assistance   help *(abstract noun)*

assistant   helper *(adjective)*

astronaut   traveller in space

audience   people who watch, e.g. a play, sporting event

bad-tempered   becoming angry or annoyed easily

balance   to keep your body steady without falling over

battered   old and slightly damaged

believe   to think that something is true

beneath   under

birds   animals with feathers and wings

blow up   to explode

bought   past tense of *buy* – get something in exchange for money

brilliance   great brightness *(abstract noun)*

brilliant   1 very bright *(adjective)*
2 wonderful; really good *(adjective)*

bristles   short, stiff hairs

camp   place where people go for a holiday and often stay in tents

canoed   travelled by canoe

captain   person in charge of a ship

capture   catch

catalogue   book which has pictures of things people can buy

caught   past tense of *catch* – to get hold of

cautious   careful

cave   large hole in the side of a hill or mountain

certainly   definitely; without doubt

civilisation   a large group of people with their own way of life

clearing   an area in a forest where there are no trees or bushes

cobwebs   a spider's web

collection	a group of similar things which are gathered together
condenses	changes into liquid
contact	get in touch with
cooler	colder; not as warm
courageous	brave
crew	people who work on a ship
cruising	travelling at a steady speed
damaged	broken or harmed
dangerous	likely to cause harm
difference	something which makes one person or thing not the same as another (abstract noun)
different	not the same as (adjective)
disadvantage	a bad feature something has
discovered	found
disguise	change appearance to look like someone else
distance	the amount of space between two things (abstract noun)
distant	not close by (adjective)
dizzy	the feeling that things around you are spinning and that you are going to fall
droplets	very small drops of liquid
dusty	covered with dust
elegance	beauty; style (abstract noun)
elegant	beautiful; stylish (adjective)
encouraged	persuaded someone to do something
engine	machine which uses energy to work
enormous	very big
equipment	things needed for a particular activity
escape	get free
evaporation	process where a liquid becomes a gas/vapour
exhausted	extremely tired
expensive	costs a lot of money; not cheap
experimenting	trying out new ideas
explorer	someone who travels to new places to find out about them
facilities	places provided for people to use
famous	well known
fantastic	really good
fascinating	extremely interesting
fetch	to collect
fiery	very bright and hot
flows	moving all the time
forms	makes
fortune-teller	someone who thinks they know what is going to happen in the future
fracture	break
free	not in prison
frowned	an expression of the face that showed the person was annoyed
gigantic	very big
gloomy	dark
guide	someone who shows you where to go
guilty	having done something wrong
hair	thing which grows on the head

harbour	area of water next to land where boats can stop
hare	animal like a rabbit
hatch	door way
hazardous	dangerous
headings	titles at the top of pages or paragraphs
heavily	a lot
high	opposite of low
hole	a space dug in the ground
hopeless	not good at
huge	very big
importance	something to be treated seriously (abstract noun)
important	serious (adjective)
immediately	straight away
incredible	difficult to believe
industries	places that produce things for sale
initial	at the beginning
inspection	a process of checking things carefully
intelligence	the ability to understand things (abstract noun)
intelligent	good at understanding (adjective)
knelt	past tense of kneel
landscape	large area of land; how the land looks
leaflet	a printed sheet of paper that gives information about something
lifeboat	small boat for getting off a large boat which is in trouble
liquid	not solid; something which can flow, e.g. water

literature	stories, poems and plays
location	the place where something is
loneliness	being alone, with no friends
maid	a woman whose job is to clean rooms in a hotel or large house
mankind	all the people on Earth
marvellous	very enjoyable
massive	very large
masts	tall poles that sails hang from
material	cloth
maze	paths with tall walls on either side which is difficult to find your way out of
meat	something you eat
meet	to come together
melting	turning into liquid
mission	important work
mixture	two or more different things put together
monsoon	a time of heavy rain in India and South East Asia
moss	a soft green plant that grows on wet ground, rocks or trees
muddle	jumble; not well ordered
mystery	a secret; unexplained (noun)
mysterious	very strange (adjective)
mumbling	speaking softly to yourself so no-one else can hear
nerve	part of the body that carries messages between the brain and the sense organs, e.g. eyes, ears
obedient	to do as you are told

obedience	doing what someone tells you to do (noun)
opinion	what you think of something
orange	1 a fruit *(noun)*
	2 between red and yellow in colour *(adjective)*
outside	opposite of inside
overboard	over a ship's side
pair	a set of two
palm trees	tropical tree with wide leaves
panic	a sudden strong feeling of worry or fear that makes you unable to think clearly or calmly
particles	very small piece of something
patient	to be able to wait for a long time and not get angry
pear	a fruit
perfect	without any faults; as good as it can be
persuade	to make someone agree to do something by giving them reasons why they should
pile	a number of things that are put on top of one another
plains	large flat areas of land
plant	1 something which grows in soil and has leaves *(noun)*
	2 to put a plant in the soil to grow *(verb)*
plenty	a lot; enough
pluck	to pull the string of a musical instrument

point of view	the way you judge a situation, according to your opinion
polluted	made dirty, spoilt or damaged
population	the number of people who live in a place
positive	showing something as good
powdery	fine and dry like powder
preceded	went in front (of someone)
precious	very valuable
prepare	to get ready ahead of time
prevented	stopped
preview	to look at something before anyone else can see it
pride	feeling of pleasure at having done something
problem	something you have to solve
promise	when you say you will definitely do something
propped open	used something to keep a door open
protected	looked after; made sure no-one damaged something
protection	process of keeping someone or something safe
provided	given
realised	knew and understood something
recycle	to use something again, often for a different purpose
reduced	made smaller or made less

reins	leather straps fixed to a horse's head and used to guide it
reply	answer
report	a written description of a subject
reward	something good you receive because of something good you have done
right	opposite of left
rough	opposite of smooth; not gentle
scorching	moving very quickly
screen	flat, glass surface on a television
sea	large area of salt water
searched	looked everywhere
secretive	not telling people things
see	notice with the eyes
several	more than two or three, but not many
shipwreck	an accident in which a ship is destroyed during a journey
shivering	shaking because you are cold or frightened
shuddered	shook several times because you were cold or frightened
shuffling	walking without lifting your feet
sigh	a long soft sound
signalled	sent a message to
silence	complete quiet (abstract noun)
silent	not making any noise (adjective)
sketch	a simple drawing done quickly (noun)

snatch	to pull or to take something away quickly
snorted	made a sudden, loud noise through the nose
soaring	flying high
solved	found the answer to
sound	1 the noise something makes (abstract noun)
	2 in good condition (adjective)
sound wave	When something makes a sound, the noise makes the air vibrate. These vibrations, are called sound waves.
souvenir	something to remind you of a person or place
space-man	astronaut
spotlight	powerful light which shines on a small part of the stage
spray	cover with small drops of liquid
stack	put one thing on top of another
staggered	walked in an uncontrolled way, as if you were going to fall over
standpipe	a tap from which you can get clean water
stream	a small river
struggling	using your strength to fight against someone or something
study	look at something closely and carefully
suitable	right; fitting
supervised	watched over
supper	an evening meal
surface	the top or outside part of something
survivor	someone who is still alive

swallow	when you eat food you swallow it
swan	a large white bird with a long neck that lives near water
swarm	a large group of insects flying together
swifter	more quickly
tanner	someone who makes animal skins into leather
tannery	the place where a tanner works
three-dimensional	not flat, but able to be measured in height, depth and width
tough	not afraid of anything
travel	to move from one place to another
unsolved	opposite of solved
vague	not clear
vein	thin tube in your body that carries blood to your heart
vibrate	to shake very quickly with small movements
violence	strong force which often causes damage *(abstract noun)*
violent	strong; forceful *(adjective)*
voyage	long journey by water
wake	track made behind a ship, plane or rocket
wallet	something to keep money in (like a purse)
warm	pleasantly hot
warn	to tell someone of a danger or problem

wasp	a black and yellow flying insect that can sting you
watch	1 look at *(verb)* 2 something which tells the time *(noun)*
water vapour	water in the form of a gas
wax	sticky material
weighed	had a weight of
whizz	move quickly with a hissing sound
whole	all of
window-pane	the glass in a window
wispy	long and thin
worried	nervous and upset
write	use a pen or pencil to make words

Thesaurus page

afraid	scared, frightened (opposite: **unafraid**)
amazing	wonderful, exciting (opposite: **dull**)
ashamed	embarrassed (opposite: **proud**)
bad-tempered	angry, annoyed, irritable, cross (opposite: **good-tempered**)
calm	peaceful (opposite: **rough**)
carefully	cautiously (opposite: **carelessly**)
clever	quick, intelligent (opposite: **stupid**)
collect	gather (opposite: **separate**)
comfortable	pleasant (opposite: **uncomfortable**)
expensive	dear (opposite: **cheap**)
fetch	carry, collect, bring (opposite: **take**)
finished	ended, stopped (opposite: **started**)
fluid	liquid (opposite: **solid**)
frowned	scowled, glared (opposite: **smiled**)
giant	huge (opposite: **small**)
glared	frowned (opposite: **smiled**)
gloomy	dark, dim (opposite: **light**)
good	1　well-behaved (opposite: **naughty**)
	2　excellent (opposite: **poor**)
	3　high quality (opposite: **bad**)
guide	leader (opposite: **follower**)
hazardous	dangerous (opposite: **safe**)
liquid	fluid, juice (opposite: **solid**)
mumbling	murmuring, muttering (opposite: **shouting**)
perfect	just right (opposite: **imperfect**)
polluted	dirty, unclean, foul (opposite: **clean**)
preceded	went in front (opposite: **came after**)
struggling	fighting, striving (opposite: **giving in**)
tiny	very small (opposite: **huge**)
well	healthy (opposite: **ill**)
wide	broad (opposite: **narrow**)

Macmillan Education
Between Towns Road, Oxford OX4 3PP
A division of Macmillan Publishers Limited
Companies and representatives throughout the world

ISBN 978-1-4050-8131-3

Design and layout by Wild Apple Design Ltd.
Illustrated by Beth Aulton, Barking Dog Art, Carlos Avalone, Juliet Breese, Kate Davies, Katy Jackson, and Mike Spoor
Cover design by Oliver Design

Printed and bound in Malaysia

2017 2016 2015 2014 2013
17 16 15 14 13 12 11 10 9

The author and publishers are grateful for permission to reprint the following copyright material.
Extract from *The Quest* (Macmillan Guided Reader) by Mandy Loader (Macmillan Heinemann ELT, 1999), copyright © Mandy Loader 1999, reprinted by permission of the author.
Judith Nicholls 'Water's for…', copyright © Judith Nicholls 1988 from *My Blue Poetry Book: This Morning My Dad Shouted* edited by Moira Andrew (Macmillan Education, 1988), reprinted by permission of the author.
Extract from *Cliffhanger* by Jacqueline Wilson (Corgi Yearling, 1995), copyright © Jacqueline Wilson 1995, reprinted by permission of The Random House Group Ltd.
Peter Thabit Jones 'I Want to be an Astronaut', copyright © Peter Thabit Jones 1992 from Scholastic Collections: Poetry edited by Wes Magee (Scholastic Books, 2006), reprinted by permission of the author.
Howard Sergeant 'Soft Landings', copyright © Howard Sergeant 1986 from *Poetry 1: The First Lick of the Lolly* edited by Moira Andrew (Macmillan Education, 1986), reprinted by permission of Cherrill Sands.
Alan Bold 'The Dolphin', copyright © Alice Bold 1984 from *A Very First Poetry Book* compiled by John Foster (Oxford University Press, 1984), reprinted by permission of Alice Bold.
Extract from *Living Earth: The Stream* by David Hunt (Macmillan Education, 1996), reprinted by permission of the publisher.
The Litter Song by Andrew Jackson copyright © Andrew Jackson 1994, taken from *Scholastic Collections* (Scholastic Ltd, 1994), reprinted by permission of the author.
Extract from *Hop Step Jump: Chichi and the Termites* by Wendy Ijioma (Macmillan Education, 2000), reprinted by permission of the publisher.
Adapted extract from 'A Night in the Jungle' from *Old Mali and the Boy* by Denis Ronald (Victor Gollancz, 1964), copyright Denis Ronald 1964, reprinted by permission of A M Heath and Company Ltd.
Jo Peters 'My Hands', copyright © Jo Peters 2000 from *The Works* edited by Paul Cookson (Macmillan Children's Books, 2000), reprinted by permission of the author.

Photo Credits
Alamy/AllOver Photolibrary p33 (tr), Alamy/Andre Jenny p150 (tl), Alamy/Andre Jenny p93 (cr), Alamy/Bubbles Photolibrary p115 (c), Alamy/Chuck Pefley p115 (t), Alamy/Danita Delimont p39 (c), Alamy/David Lyons p116 (t), Alamy/David R Frazier Photolibrary Inc p150 br), Alamy/David Tipling p65 (br),
Alamy/Foodfolio (tr & cr), Alamy/Garden World p150 (cl), Alamy/Glen Allison p98 (b), Alamy/Harold R Stinnette p39 (r), Alamy/Image State p117 (t), Alamy/Jeff Greenberg p132 (t), Alamy/Joe Fox p32 (bc), Alamy/John Pickles p32 (c), Alamy/John Terence Turner p32 (r), Alamy/Kim Westerskov p65 (cr), Alamy/Luca Mion (bc), Alamy/Lyndon Beddoe p150 (c), Alamy/Mark Levy p65 (c), Alamy/Medicolor p109 (tr), Alamy/Michael Jenner p49, Alamy/Mike Kipling Photography p32 (tc), Alamy/Network Photographers p93 (br), Alamy/Nicholas Frost p54, Alamy/PCL p97, Alamy/Petr Svarc p96 (b), Alamy/Photofusion p30 (l), Alamy/Photolibrary Wales p33 (tl), Alamy/Popperfoto p72, Alamy/Profimedia CZ sro p108 (c), Alamy/Profimedia.CZ sro p32 (cr), Alamy/RF p150 (tc), Alamy/Rhinofilm p33 (b), Alamy/Robert Harding Picture Library p108 (t), Alamy/Seb Rogers p30 (r), Alamy/Stock Connection Distribution p24 (r), Alamy/This Life Pictures p150 (b), Alamy/Visual Arts Library (London) p116 (b), Corbis/Ariel Skelley p32 (cl), Corbis/Bohemian Nomad Picturemakers p98 (t), Corbis/Galen Rowell p24 (l), Corbis/Kevin Schafer p96 (tl), Corbis/Paul Linse p115 (b), Corbis/Massimo Mastrorillo p93 (br), Corbis/Paul A Souders p92 (br), Corbis/Robert Gill;Papilio p93 (c), Corbis/Roger Ressmeyer p74 (tr), Corbis/Tom Stewart p39 (br), Corbis/Wolfgang Deuter/Zefa p92 (cr), Empics p31, Getty Images p 33 (c), Getty Images/David Woodfall p108 (b), Getty Images/Fran Lemmens p150 (tl), Getty Images/National Geographic p30 (cl), Getty Images/National Geographic/Roy Toft p32 (br), Getty Images/Scott Neville p109 (tl), Hearthland Images/Photographers Direct p30 (cr), Hearthland Images/Photographers Direct p24 (cr), Joe Fox Photography/Photographers Direct p32 (bl), Keith Glover Photography/Photographers Direct p127 (t & b), Keith Glover Photography/Photographers Direct p142 (r), Macmillan RF p117 (b), Macmillan RF p17 (br), Macmillan RF p17 (tl), Macmillan RF p24 (cl), Macmillan RF p39 (tr), Photofusion/Photographers Direct p142 (l), Science & Society Picture Library p126 (br), Science Photo Library p126 (bl), Science Photo Library/Alan Sirulnikoff p17 (tr), Science Photo Library/Astrid & Hanns-Frieder Michler p65 (tl), Science Photo Library/Dr Dan Sudia p17 (cl), Science Photo Library/Eye of Science p65 (tr), Science Photo Library/Mike Agliolo p17 (bl), Science Photo Library/NASA p67, Science Photo Library/NASA p69, Science Photo Library/Nasa p74 (cr & b), Science Photo Library/Pascal Goetgheluck p19 (t), Science Photo Library/Roger Harris p74 (c), Science Photo Library/Sinclair Stammers p77, Still Pictures/Cyril Ruoso p112, TP Photography/Photographers Direct p32 (tr)